Better Homes and Gardens®
QUICK & EASY
curb appeal

WILEY

John Wiley & Sons, Inc

For general information about our other products and services, please contact our Customer Care Department within the United States at (800) 762-2974, outside the United States at (317) 572-3993 or fax (317) 572-4002.

Wiley also publishes its books in a variety of electronic formats. Some content that appears in print may not be available in electronic books. For more information about Wiley products, visit our web site at www.wiley.com.

ISBN 978-0-470-61277-4

Printed in the United States of America

10 9 8 7 6 5 4 3 2 1

Note to the Readers:
Due to differing conditions, tools, and individual skills, John Wiley & Sons, Inc., assumes no responsibility for any damages, injuries suffered, or losses incurred as a result of following the information published in this book. Before beginning any project, review the instructions carefully, and if any doubts or questions remain, consult local experts or authorities. Because codes and regulations vary greatly, you always should check with authorities to ensure that your project complies with all applicable local codes and regulations. Always read and observe all of the safety precautions provided by manufacturers of any tools, equipment, or supplies, and follow all accepted safety procedures.

Welcome

What makes great curb appeal? Interestingly enough, you know it when you see it. That two-story house down the block with the pretty arbor and beautiful stone walkway; or the pretty little cottage your drive past on the way to work with all the amazing flowers. These are houses that seem to shine with personality and character—nice landscaping, compelling colors, perhaps an outstanding detail or two. Above all, they're well-cared-for properties that glow with pride of ownership.

Having wonderful curb appeal isn't magic; it's simply a continual process of refinement, updating, and regular maintenance. It's many smaller elements, added as time and budget allow, working together to create a harmonious whole. Most important, curb appeal is much more than good looks—it's about preserving the value of your home investment.

Better Homes and Gardens® Quick & Easy Curb Appeal is designed to help you make your home the best it can be. Each chapter offers helpful hints, easy-to-accomplish projects, and beautiful images that show you dozens of simple ways to add curb appeal. Whether it's sprucing up your front door, choosing trim colors, or simply patching the lawn, you'll find plenty of information and inspiration on the pages that follow.

Contents

CHAPTER ONE

Curb Appeal at a Glance

WE OFTEN SAY A HOUSE HAS CURB APPEAL when we think that it's especially good-looking. The truth is that good curb appeal is much more than an eye-catching color scheme or a pretty flowering tree. It's usually the result of thoughtful planning and diligent maintenance on the part of the homeowners.

This care and attention to detail has its rewards. Pride of ownership is certainly an important benefit, but there's more. A house with curb appeal is likely to retain its value and protect your investment. In fact, professional appraisers are apt to reduce the assigned value of a poorly maintained house and property by as much as 10 percent. When it comes time to sell, a house with strong curb appeal is much more likely to receive serious offers in comparison to other houses of similar price.

Fortunately, great curb appeal doesn't necessarily come from sweeping changes and major renovations. Small changes—a brick planter and a dash of colorful flowers—go a long way toward establishing powerful curb appeal. See for yourself. On the next few pages, we've pointed out some of the special touches and interesting details that add up to wonderful curb appeal. The rest of this book is devoted to showing you simple curb appeal ideas that can help you make your house and property as appealing as it can be.

1. **An ornamental tree helps frame the entryway to the house.**
2. **A hanging flower basket brings a splash of color.**
3. **A seating area is an invitation to visit.**
4. **Movable container planters put color where you want it.**
5. **Brick steps add visual interest.**
6. **A curving walkway draws the eye.**
7. **Planting beds with brick edgings provide the yard with texture.**

The best curb appeal happens when the many elements of a house and yard work together. Such thoughtful planning doesn't mean expensive details or ambitious landscaping projects. For this single-story, shingle-sided home, a strong white accent color ties everything together—window trim, railing along the outdoor porch, rafter tails and fascia, garage doors, and even the front gate have been given a bright white coat of paint. All the other elements, such as the curving stone path, the many plantings, and the grey body color of the house, are gathered together by the bold white accents. As a final touch, ornamental shrubs feature an assortment of fine white flowers.

1. **Custom hardware gives the garage doors the appearance of double-swinging entry doors.**
2. **Custom grilles bring a touch of style to the windows.**
3. **The grey body color with white trim is strong but not overpowering.**
4. **Curbside flower beds contrast with the well-trimmed lawn and overall neat appearance.**
5. **Stone pavers are matched by a stone planter and stone-clad lamp posts flanking the gate.**
6. **A classic white gate announces the entry to the property.**
7. **Entryway lighting is good-looking and adds safety at night.**

This quiet suburban house displays self-assured curb appeal with a well-orchestrated mix of color and architectural detail. Although the colors are not bold, the subtle mix of creamy yellow painted brick siding, white trim, blue-green shutters, and gable ends stained a soft grey presents a textured palette that's both compelling and soothing. Repeating geometrical grids at the windows, doors, and along the porch serve to unify the look while giving the house its own distinct personality.

1. **Introducing a new hue at the gable ends is one way to vary the overall paint scheme.**
2. **Trimwork between the porch posts is an easy way to establish architectural interest.**
3. **Contrasting shutters provide light touches of color.**
4. **An all-glass front door is a stylish welcome for visitors.**
5. **Movable pots add dashes of color at the entry steps.**
6. **Grooves cut into the concrete walkway give the appearance of flagstone.**
7. **Simple plantings hide the foundation walls.**

CHAPTER TWO

Beautiful Lawns

NOTHING SETS OFF YOUR HOME like a lush, green lawn. A great lawn is inviting, complements your house and landscaping, and sets the stage for great curb appeal. It also suggests that the rest of your home is just as beautifully maintained. A well-cared-for lawn doesn't just look good, it creates an ideal surface for children to play on and extends your outdoor living space. A quality lawn is like a welcome mat that'll make you want to pull out some lawn chairs and invite the neighbors over to chat and relax.

But if your lawn looks a little shabby, with brown spots and patches of weeds, the appearance of your entire property suffers. Fortunately, a little care and routine maintenance will ensure that your lawn remains green, healthy, and a point of pride for your house. Regular mowing, watering, fertilizing, weeding control, and a little reseeding now and again will do wonders.

Understanding about different types of grasses and how to care for them helps make lawn care easier. Knowing how grasses respond to heat, cold, and moisture is an easy way to make sure your lawn stays in peak condition.

If you're lucky enough to already have a great lawn, read on to find out how to keep it that way. If your lawn is struggling a bit, it's not difficult to build it back up. Follow these simple tips for a year or two and you'll have a lawn that will have the neighbors asking how you keep your lawn in such perfect shape!

Although it's natural to look at this beautiful front landscape and be drawn to the flowers, ornamental trees, and charming arbor, the scene would not be so impressive without the wide expanse of carefully tended lawn. Lawns are the visual anchor of any good landscaping plan and are essential to creating great curb appeal.

Knowing Your Grasses

Grasses are divided into two groups: Cool-season grasses, grown in roughly the northern half of the U.S. and the Pacific Northwest, and warm-season grasses, grown in the southern half. How you mow, fertilize, and control weeds depends on which category your grass or blend of grasses falls into.

• Cool-season grasses are noted for their fine, soft texture and deep, shiny green blades. But they also need lots of water and don't tolerate extended heat well. They include annual ryegrass, fine fescues, Kentucky bluegrass, perennial ryegrass, and tall fescue. When starting from seed, it's preferable to plant cool-season grasses in fall but spring will also work.

• Warm-season grasses are coarser, but are better suited to hot and/or dry conditions. They include bahiagrass, bermudagrass, buffalograss, centipede grass, and zoysiagrass. Warm-season grass seed should be planted in spring or early summer.

Not sure what you have in your lawn right now? Many lawn care services will do a free evaluation. They can also inform you about the best grasses for your particular region.

Is a Lawn Service for You?

The answer: It's definitely worth investigating. Start by measuring your yard to figure out how many square feet you have. Then go to the garden center and price out a year's worth of fertilizer and weed killer. (A knowledgeable clerk can help you do this.) Include any special equipment you would need to purchase, such as a spreader or sprayer. Then call three lawn care services and ask them the pricing of their annual fertilizer-herbicide program. Because of volume, their prices may be surprisingly close to what you'd spend at the garden center. Bonus: You won't have to remember what to put on when, or find the time to do it. You'll never have a bag of lawn fertilizer in your garage, gathering dust, again!

A healthy lawn sets the stage for a landscape scheme that steps up by degrees toward the strong architectural lines of this two-story home.

Good to Know: How to start a new lawn from seed

Starting a lawn from seed is far more economical than sod. A small lawn can be started with as little as $20 of seed. Follow planting times on packages exactly. It's important to start with a weed-free area and good soil. Kill weeds as needed with a nonselective herbicide spray. Wait three days. Then spread sand, compost, and other soil amendments generously. Also spread a lawn starter fertilizer, according to package directions.

Rake as evenly as possible. Then use a roller to further smooth and firm the soil. Spread seed with a hopper, following package directions. Lightly rake the soil surface to mix the soil. Then mulch the seedbed with straw or burlap and water well. Water daily until the grass is approximately 1 inch high. Then cut back on watering. Mow once grass is 3 inches high.

Rejuvenating a Tired Lawn

If your lawn is looking spare or heavy foot traffic or other damage has taken its toll, it's time for little renovation work. Lawn repair is inexpensive and takes just minutes, and can transform a problem lawn into a beautiful lawn. All you need is a little grass seed or sod.

Rejuvenate warm-season grasses (page 14) in the spring and early summer. Rejuvenate cool-season grasses (page 14) preferably in early fall, but spring will also work. Follow-up watering is critical. Keep new seed or sod moist for a week or two after installation to assure that the new grass gets a healthy start.

One of the easiest ways to make a sparse lawn fuller is by overseeding. Pull or spray problem weeds with a nonselective weed killer. Wait three days, then rake up any dead or damaged grass with a ground rake. Sprinkle grass seed over the entire area, or over the entire lawn. (Use just your hand in small areas a few feet across. Use a spreader in large areas.)

Rake in lightly and tamp down seed onto the soil as best you can. Water in well, or time it right before a gentle rain. Water again daily for the next week or two to assure good germination.

QUICK APPEAL:

Want to fertilize your lawn without chemicals? Each spring and each fall, spread ¼ inch of compost on top of the grass and rake in gently. You'll improve soil quality and decrease thatch to boot. Or check out the growing assortment of organic lawn fertilizers now available at garden centers and through professional lawn services.

How to Repair a Lawn with Sod

1. Dig up sod from a landscaping project elsewhere in your yard or purchase sod from a landscaper. Dig out the problem area to the same depth as the piece of sod. Work a soil amendment, such as compost, into the bare area.

2. Cut the sod to fit with a small saw, large knife, or spade. Fit the sod in tightly, making sure ends butt up against each other to prevent drying out. If necessary, fill any gaps with soil. Tamp down sod lightly by walking on it.

3. Water well. Soak the soil under the sod 4 to 6 inches. (Pull up sod and use a stick or trowel to check.) Keep sod moist for the next two weeks until established.

How to Patch a Lawn

1. Locate bare or damaged spots in your lawn. They may be unsightly, but you can fix them in minutes and for just a few dollars by scattering a little seed.

2. Remove any existing weeds and rake the soil to rough it up and loosen it so the seed doesn't wash or blow away. Dig in any soil amendments, such as compost, now.

3. Top with topsoil. Alternatively, you can also top the area (especially if it's lower than the surrounding lawn) with purchased topsoil or potting soil. Rake the area smooth so it's even with the surrounding soil.

4. Sprinkle grass seed over the area and gently "fluff" the soil to distribute the seed. Lawn patch products, such as the one shown here, are ideal since they include moisture-conserving mulch that protects the seed and adds nutrients. The mulch breaks down over time.

5. Water gently but well. The water should go down about 2 inches into the soil. (Mark off the area with stakes and string, if needed, to prevent foot traffic.) Water daily for the next two weeks until the grass is 1-inch high.

Proper Mowing and Watering

While most people don't necessarily give much thought to proper mowing and watering techniques, a few simple guidelines can do wonders for the look and health of your lawn all during the outdoor season. Once you get into the habit of following these simple methods, you'll find the results are worth the little bit of extra time it takes to have a great lawn.

GOOD MOWING TECHNIQUES:

• **Keep mower blades sharp.** Sharpen them 1 to 3 times a growing season. Dull blades tear the grass leaf, making it ragged, promoting uneven healing, and giving a beige cast to your lawn.

• **Mow high.** It keeps turf healthy and shades the ground, preventing weeds and keeping soil moist. Mow cool-season grasses, such as Kentucky bluegrass, $2\frac{1}{2}$ inches high. Mow most warm-season grasses at 1 to 2 inches.

• **Mow frequently.** As a rule of thumb, you should never remove more than one-third of the leaf blade because it stresses the grass.

• **Use a mulching mower, if possible.** Not only does it eliminate bagging, the microshredded bits of leaves act as an excellent mulch and can prevent thatch. They then break down and feed the soil. If you don't have a mulching mower, outfit your current mower with a mulching blade for a similar effect.

WATER SMARTER:

• **Never water when it's hot or windy.** The best time to water is right before sunup, when the weather tends to be still. (Set a timer.) Then the moisture can dry off quickly once the sun is up, preventing wet leaves that promote fungal diseases.

• **Water deep and seldom, rather than frequently and shallow.** Deep watering encourages roots to grow farther, where they'll find yet more moisture. Turf needs 1 inch of water a week. Measure this by setting a shallow dish out in the yard when you water. When it has 1 inch of water in it, you know you're done. (This usually takes several hours.)

• **Consider an irrigation system.** Yes, they're expensive. But they are also extremely efficient and use minimal water for maximum effect. In the western half of the U.S., an irrigation system is almost a must for a truly healthy, thick lawn.

Keep your mower in good working order with simple annual maintenance that includes changing the engine oil and replacing the air filter. Two or three times each mowing season disconnect the spark plug and tilt the mower on its side to remove clogged grass and debris from the underside of the deck.

Water your lawn if soil begins to dry out and before grass starts to wilt. If footprints on the lawn remain visible instead of bouncing right back, that's an indication it's time to give your lawn a good soaking.

Good to Know: Made for the shade

If your grass is struggling under a tree, consider groundcover instead. Healthy turf needs at least 8 hours of full, unfiltered sun a day—ideally more. Shade-tolerant blends need only slightly less—perhaps an hour. Also, the roots of many trees, especially maples and evergreens, suck moisture and nutrients away from turf and make mowing difficult.

So rather than fight a losing battle, consider planting that shady area with a groundcover. A thick stand of healthy groundcover is far more beautiful than a path of struggling turf. Consider perennial vinca minor, bishops-weed, liriope, pachysandra, ivy, and more.

CHAPTER **THREE**

Plantings

WHEN YOU'RE LOOKING TO ENHANCE CURB APPEAL, proper plantings are essential to add beauty and personality to the landscape. Well-chosen trees, shrubs, perennials, and annuals add texture, depth, color, and character to a home. Conversely, if your plantings are struggling, it sends a message that basic maintenance and care are lacking—factors that may affect the value of your property.

To assess your plantings, step across the street and take a look at how healthy your plantings appear, and whether any trees or shrubs need trimming or should be removed altogether. Your plantings should be in scale with the house and blend into the overall appearance of your property. Pay special attention to the relationship between plantings and the doors and windows of your house. Plantings that obscure doors and windows might seem to create privacy, but they can obscure key architectural features and block light from entering your home.

Plantings should be placed so it's easy for visitors to figure out where the main entrance is located. Pairs of ornamental trees or tall shrubs, positioned at either side of an entryway, help define the beginning of a walkway and indicate the way to your front door.

Plantings also should fit the character and style of the house. Imagine horizontal and vertical lines running from the plantings, and assess how well those enhance the angles of the house. Eliminating or fixing problem plantings and then adding new ones are excellent, economical ways to improve the public appearance of your home.

Try a mix of evergreens, trees, shrubs, perennials, and annuals to add life and texture and set your home apart from the pack. Start with a row of foundation plantings along the front. Then add small trees and a few colorful accent shrubs. Finish off the planting scheme with several drifts of long-blooming perennials and several clusters of bright annuals in the ground or in pots.

You'll find that your modest investment of time and money will pay off big time in a home that looks beautifully groomed and thoughtfully landscaped.

Well-structured flower beds border this corner property with color. The low plantings help place emphasis on the strong architectural lines of the house. Accent trees placed well to the edges of the main line of sight neatly frame the property.

Front Yard Essentials

Your plantings are essential elements of your front yard. For successful curb appeal, all the elements should be considered together. When planning plantings for your front yard, make sure planting beds and key landscape elements, such as trees and shrubs, enhance the natural features of your yard and help emphasize walkways, your entry, and the character of your yard, whether it's formal or casual. Here are guidelines to consider when deciding on plantings:

• **Create a direct route** by establishing a simple path to your front door. Planting beds along your walkway helps define the starting point of a walkway and its edges. Overly winding paths obscured by overhanging plants or creeping ground covers have a certain appeal—to a point. But make sure plants along your walkways are well trimmed and easy to walk around. There should be room for two people to walk side-by-side; generally, 42 to 48 inches is enough width.

• **Remember your own views.** A front garden must have stellar curb appeal, but it needs to look wonderful from inside the house, too. The view of the garden from inside the house is often forgotten as the landscape is designed. Gaze out each window that will overlook your plantings as you begin designing your outside space. Note where you eyes land, and consider creating a focal point there.

• **Make a place for sitting.** Include space in the front yard for chairs or benches; you'll be more inclined to enjoy the wonderful space you have created.

• **Let your personality shine through** by adding personal touches to your space. Be sure to include your favorite plants, garden ornaments, and even family mementos, such as favorite rocks or seashells collected on family vacations.

USE CURVES AND COLORS

A gently winding path is the perfect entrance into this front yard. Flanked by a colorful bed of blooming annuals, it looks great all through the seasons. Planters brighten up a chimney near the front door, and a wide terrace creates a perfect spot for entertaining.

TRY A CLASSIC LOOK

A picket fence surrounds this dooryard and makes a great backdrop for a summer show of purple delphinium and a rainbow of ranunculus. The cottage-style planting is repeated along the foundation.

MAKE A BOUNDARY

Blooms planted in a cottage garden right beside the sidewalk allow passersby to enjoy the flowers up close. Tuck fragrant plants, such as roses, lilies, and herbs, along walkways for extra sensory appeal.

LOSE YOUR LAWN

Enhance a rustic or Arts and Crafts home with a rugged walkway of pavers broken up by pockets of low-growing ground cover, such as this sweet alyssum. Lush plantings on both sides of the path help prevent this small-space front yard from feeling too tiny.

TRY A DRAMATIC COLOR COMBO

Here's another example of using color effectively. Bright red bougainvilleas clothe the front porch while white marguerite daisies and blue lobelia playfully cloak the front walk. Yellow pansies add a bit of extra sparkle.

Creating Layers with Plantings

QUICK APPEAL:

Stumped on what shapes and sizes of plantings your home needs? Take a picture! Stand on your front sidewalk or across the street and snap away with your digital camera. Then print the images and draw improvements right on top of them with a marker, adding or subtracting trees and shrubs, planters and pots. Make fresh printouts as needed and keep drawing until you get the right combination of plantings.

Beautiful plantings with great curb appeal are the result of careful planning. Fortunately, the process isn't difficult. Simply think about planting in layers, with each layer adding different amounts of color and texture to your yard. Understanding how each layer plays an important role is the first step toward creating plantings that you'll be proud of for years to come.

Layer One: Foundation Plantings

These are the workhorses of the landscape. Although foundation plantings typically aren't very showy, they perform an important job. They're planted next to the house to soften the hard edges of the building with greenery, visually integrating the structure into the landscape.

Evergreen shrubs, such as yews and boxwood, are classic foundation plantings. They look good even in winter in cold climates. Plant foundation plantings all of one type, all in a row, or mix up different shrubs.

Position foundation shrubs carefully. It's a common mistake to plant them too close to the house. Check the label for mature width and position accordingly. Shrubs should be positioned so when full-grown they stop short of the house a few inches. At the corner of the house, choose tall shrubs or low trees to soften those areas. Again, choose types that have greenery or interesting bark all year long.

Layer Two: Accent Trees

Trees give height, cooling shade, and character to a yard. Keep in mind the ultimate height and width of the tree and mark on the ground before planting. Accent trees grow 15 to 25 feet high, so they set off your home rather than overwhelm it. Look for trees that have four seasons of interest, such as spring flowers, attractive summer foliage, colorful fall foliage, and an interesting bark or shape in winter. Usually, just one or two will add the height and color you're looking for.

This profusion of plantings may seem untamed, but directly in front of the house it is deliberately scaled to be under about four feet tall to allow the cheery red door to mark the entryway. Taller plantings and an arbor for climbing plants have been positioned off to one side.

Layer Three: Accent Shrubs

Shrubs come in a wide range of sizes, from just a few inches high to 12 feet tall, and have a variety of shapes. Many varieties boast interesting leaves or showy or fragrant flowers. Cluster several accent shrubs around trees, around foundation plantings, or in beds or borders. Shrubs of any sort seldom look good planted all by their lonesome, out in the middle of a lawn.

Layer Four: Perennials

Usually growing just a few inches to a few feet high, perennials add color and fragrance for a few weeks. Since their bloom time is limited, choose perennials, such as daylilies or Siberian irises, that have foliage that looks good even when the plant isn't in bloom. Except for large perennials, such as peonies, most perennials are best displayed in plantings of six or more for stronger impact. Scattering and mixing perennials can create a messy patchwork effect.

Framed by large, older trees, this comfortable suburban house is well suited to entryway plantings that lead visitors directly to the front door. Low boxwood hedges to either side of the steps lend a touch of formality to the structured arrangement of plants.

Layer Five: Annuals

Annuals add bolts of color wherever you need them, whether in pots, planters, baskets, beds, or borders. Cool-season annuals, such as pansies, snapdragons, and annual lobelia, can take light frosts and so are ideal for winter plantings in mild-winter areas. Use them for early spring plantings in cold-winter areas. When cool-season annuals are done blooming, replace with showy warm-season annuals, which can't tolerate any frosts but love summer heat, such as marigolds, impatiens, and petunias. They'll bloom the rest of the growing season until fall frost.

When choosing plantings, keep in mind the colors of your home's exterior. Flowers and foliage close to the house need to coordinate with the main house color. Almost all colors look good paired with a house featuring a neutral white or gray base color, for example. Conversely, a house featuring a strong base color can be complemented by green foliage and low-key flowers. Try to avoid repeating similar colors. Red flowers against a red brick house, for example, can simply get lost.

If your house is green, look for variegated foliage in plants, or foliage in deep purple-greens or bright yellow-greens to contrast with the siding of the house. When coordinating planting colors, don't forget any accent colors on the house. The color of doors, shutters, window boxes, and trimwork also comes into play.

Planting Perennials and Shrubs

1. Dig a hole a little deeper and wider than the container or root ball of the plant. This loosens the soil and allows roots to grow outward more easily. Always improve the soil when planting—add a few shovelfuls of compost. Compost feeds the plant and improves soil texture.

2. Place the plant carefully in the hole. If the plant is root-bound, with roots circling around the bottom of the pot, use a trowel or your hands to rake out the roots and loosen them, spreading them outward. Set the plant in the hole so that the level of the soil on the roots is the same as the soil around it. Fill in with soil, using your foot to tamp it

down. You want it firm but not packed hard.

3. Water the plant deeply and well, soaking the soil thoroughly several inches down. Do not fertilize at this time. Starter stimulator products usually are not necessary. Keep the soil moist for the next week or two so the plant can get established.

The Magic of Trees

Some days it's true: You think that you will never see a thing as lovely as a tree. Trees in spring can be covered with flowers or attractive catkins. In summer, they add deep green cooling shade. Many trees in fall ignite the landscape with rich sunset colors. And in winter, they provide shelter to birds, with evergreen types brightening an otherwise bleak landscape. Plus, a tree is an investment. It dominates your front yard and lasts for decades, so you'll want to choose carefully.

Trees not only look good, they make our landscapes more comfortable and the environment healthier, too. In the landscape, when placed on the west or south side of our houses, trees reduce cooling costs. The U.S. Forest Service estimates they can reduce cooling costs by 15 to 50 percent. In winter, the bare branches of deciduous types allow warming sun into our homes. Plant evergreens and other trees to the north of a house and you'll slow winter winds, keeping your home warmer and reducing heating bills by as much as 30 percent.

Trees are critical to the health of our planet. A single mature tree can absorb 48 pounds of carbon dioxide a year, releasing enough oxygen back into the atmosphere to support 2 human beings. Tree leaves absorb and filter out harmful particulates from car exhaust and other pollutants. An urban tree can remove 48 pounds of particulates from the air daily.

How to Plant a Tree

Planting a tree is a simple task that can be completed in less than an hour.

1. Dig a hole several inches deeper and wider than the pot or bag that the tree comes in. This allows the roots to grow outward more easily.

2. Add several shovelfuls of compost to enrich the soil and improve soil texture.

3. Knock or cut the tree out of its pot. If the roots are surrounded by a bag, remove the bag. If the roots have been spiraling around the bottom of the pot, loosen them with your fingers or a towel.

4. Set the tree in the planting hole. Position it so that it's as deep in the ground as it was in the pot or bag.

5. Fill in with soil, tamping down firmly with your foot. Shape a small moat around the tree for water to puddle to better water the tree.

6. Mulch with wood chip mulch about 2 inches thick, keeping the area around the base of the trunk clear. Extend the mulch out as far as the dripline of the tree. (This is a good way to protect it from mowers and string trimmers, too.)

7. Set a hose on a very slow drizzle and allow it to soak in around the tree for a half hour or longer, until the soil is drenched several inches down.

Do not fertilize the tree for at least two weeks, if at all. Also, no special starter chemicals are needed. Staking is necessary only in very windy conditions or to protect the tree from getting knocked over by machinery or children.

Ornamental Trees for Your Region

Ornamental trees can have a significant impact on the curb appeal of your home. Most varieties feature interesting leaves and eye-catching blossoms that make them the center of attention. However, you won't want to overdo it—adding one or two ornamental trees is all your front yard is likely to require. That's why it's important to do your research and make sure you select the right ornamental tree for your region—you'll want it to be healthy and good-looking for years to come.

Every tree has its advantages and disadvantages. Take time at a garden center that sells a wide variety of trees to talk with a knowledgeable clerk or manager about the best trees for your region and space. If possible, go during the week rather than the weekend when you'll get more assistance.

It's also a good idea to research online. Search "recommended trees" combined with the name of your state or region. Information from state extension services is usually the most thorough and unbiased. Look for facts about which trees are cold-hardy, drought-tolerant, and fire-safe for your area. You'll also find which trees have potential problems, like splitting under snow load, or messy fruits or seedpods that they drop, or susceptibility to local diseases and pests.

Some tried-and-true favorites with few problems include non-fruiting flowering crabapples, dogwoods, serviceberry, saucer magnolia, and oaks.

Small spaces present landscaping challenges that can be solved with ornamental trees. The front-facing courtyard shown here called for small trees to provide shade and to break up the large façade. If you're planning to add trees to a small area, be sure to evaluate both the projected height and width of your tree at maturity.

Cool Containers

One of the easiest ways to add curb appeal is with inexpensive arrangements of colorful container plantings. Simple to create—and a snap to change whenever you want—containers add color and cheer to your walkway, front steps, and entry. You can choose a pair of dramatic pots to flank your front door, or combine a variety of shapes and sizes to create an entire container garden. Either way, front yard containers say, "Welcome!"

Try some of these ideas for attractive front yard containers:

- **Start with the pots.** Go with larger rather than smaller. They need watering less often (smaller pots dry out faster) and have more impact.

- **When grouping pots,** make sure the colors and materials work together. Go for all terra-cotta pots, for example. With wood planters or boxes, paint them all the same color. Otherwise, the look can be cluttered without a unifying element.

- **Window boxes** are a sweet way to add charm to the front of a home. Choose or build a box at least as wide as the window to keep it in proportion.

- **Add hanging baskets** to bring color and softening foliage at eye level and higher. You can get extending hooks to hang them on either side of your front door, on either side of garage doors, or in a row in front of a large picture window.

- **In winter, in cold regions,** stick boughs of evergreen into window boxes, planters, or large containers for winter greenery. Accent with real or fake branches of berries.

QUICK APPEAL:

Make fast work of moving container plants by using a hand truck—the kind professional movers use for shifting appliances and other bulky items. Garden centers carry hand trucks especially designed for transporting potted garden plants.

Soften railings by planting a perennial or annual vine at the base of the steps. Clematis, morning glories, moon flower, scarlet runner bean, black-eyed Susan vine, and other medium-sized vines all work well. These pots feature a monochromatic mix of lavender and petunias.

Curb Appeal in a Box

Flower boxes are an easy way to brighten up the front of your house with color. Although the classic window box is usually placed directly underneath a window, flower boxes look great on porches, steps, or placed on a bench. Changing plants to match the seasons is a snap.

STANDING TALL

Raise your flower boxes to new heights by investing in a tiered stand. You'll squeeze in more showy greenery that you can see better from the street, and yet use very little precious porch floor space. If your porch roof casts considerable shade, rely on coleus, impatiens, ivies, houseplants, and other shady characters.

IT'S EASY TO BE GREEN

This box is large enough to blur the line between planter and window box. Crafted of wood painted deep green (an easy color to blend with a wide variety of house colors), it creates a substantial planting area by the front door. Plantings are in reds and purples, including purple fountain grass, red salvia, and deep purple-green coral bells.

LOVELY LATTICE

Add architectural interest to even the plainest of homes with a latticework window box. Simply make a lattice panel and attach it to the front of a basic box. This one is filled with asparagus fern (a great trailing plant for window boxes in light shade), Joseph's coat, and annual mums.

BENCH YOUR BOX

Not all window boxes have to be mounted to a window. Set a window box on a bench for a casual perch that shows off pretty blooms. Russet ornamental grasses and coral bells with autumn-tinged leaves tie in the orange and blue of the box with the orange of the house.

CLASSY CLASSIC

A white wood flower box is as traditional as they come, and this recessed panel design is a classic. Legs on the bottom ensure good drainage and prevent the bottom of the box (and the porch floor) from mildew and rot. The cheerful yellow mums, bright green ivy, and blue and purple pansies set off the bright color of the house.

RUGGEDLY SIMPLE

This simple box made of salvaged, weathered wood is at home in a country setting. It's planted for fall with blue fescue ornamental grass, ornamental cabbage, China asters, and pansies.

HOW LOW CAN YOU GO?

Low windows don't benefit much from window boxes since there's so little room to work with. Save time by simply setting a box directly beneath the window on the front porch floor. This hayrack planter is lined with sheet moss and filled to overflowing with sunset-colored flowers and ornamental grasses that work well with the warm color of the brick.

Designing Beds and Borders

Frame your home with color and texture by adding or improving a bed or border. Well-thought-out beds and borders can make the difference between a home that just has a yard and a home that has great curb appeal. Beds and borders are simple to establish, and they add shape, definition, and polish to a landscape.

Planting beds have different functions and roles to play in the overall appearance of your home. Knowing the various types and thinking about each type as a distinct project will help you budget effectively and make the best use of your landscaping time.

Foundation bed: This is a flower bed or border located along the foundation walls of your house. It's the perfect place to position key ornamental shrubs; just make sure your shrubbery won't rub up against your siding or obscure windows when they grow to maturity. Once you've determined locations for shrubs, fill in the rest of the bed with smaller accent shrubs, reliable perennials, or colorful annuals.

Island bed: This is a bed or border that has no physical connection to any other element in the landscape, such as another bed, a

Large flower beds, such as this six-foot-wide swath of color and texture, require careful planning so that plantings graduate in size, with shorter plants in front and taller flowers behind.

The Side Story

Side yards play an important role in curb appeal, too. It's easy for a homeowner to think of them merely as utility areas, but passersby and visitors will view them as part of the front landscape. Be sure to spruce up your side yards so they aren't undermining all your good efforts out front.

- Most side yards are transitional places used to get from one part of your yard to another. Therefore, a good path is critical. Make sure the path is in good functioning order, or create one in flagstone or gravel.

- Plant interesting landscaping that includes a small flowering tree or two. Add low-maintenance perennials or hardy ground covers.

- If your side yard is a refuge for garbage cans and other less-than-attractive necessities, erect a short length of picket fence or other screening structure. A small tree or two or a few shrubs can serve the same screening effect. Choose evergreens so they'll do their job all year round.

sidewalk, or a driveway. Often a circle, it can also be an attractive, free-form abstract shape. Set in the middle of the lawn, an island bed should be well designed to harmonize with the whole landscape. Scale the height of your plants so that at maturity they graduate in size from the front to the back of the bed when seen from the street.

Flanking borders: Planting beds along a walkway is a beautiful way to set off a front entry. Create a flower bed on one or both sides of your front walk, using reliable perennials with established personalities, such as hostas, English ivy, and shrub roses.

Make sure plantings won't intrude onto the walkway surface more than a few inches by keeping them well trimmed.

Driveway strip border: Have a narrow strip that runs alongside your driveway, backed by a fence or building? Transform it from a problem spot to a showcase by planting low-maintenance perennials. Be sure to choose types that match the available light (sun or shade). And if the plantings are likely to get foot traffic (or, worse yet, tire traffic), choose durable low-growers, like creeping thyme, creeping periwinkle, or bishop's-weed.

An Easy Stone Planter

Add architectural interest, greenery, and function to the front or side of your house with a planter bed made from brick. Design the bed so the soil doesn't exceed the height of the foundation or come within 6 inches of wood and stucco siding.

1. Create a foundation for the planter by digging out a trench. Allow 1 inch of trench for every 8 inches of height of the wall. Allow enough depth to accommodate whatever base material you will be adding. Use a string and stake to keep the trench straight.

2. Add coarse sand or gravel to a depth of about 4 inches along the length of the trench. This base material allows for drainage and gives you a firm foundation for the brick walls.

3. Pack the base material down firmly with a compactor to prevent excess settling of the planter walls.

4. Lay the stones. Depending on the design of your block, you may have certain types for the first course, as

Power Flowers

After finishing your project, it's important to give your plants the care they need so they can grow big, lush, and gorgeous. Get your plants off to a great start and help them develop healthy root systems with these essential tips:

- **Water, water, water!** Water deeply and well. In warm weather, this can mean daily, especially in very hot weather or windy conditions. If you're leaving town for a few days, be sure to arrange to have a trusted neighbor continue your watering routine.

- **Potting mixes with water-retaining crystals** are excellent at helping retain soil moisture. You may purchase crystals separately and mix in at planting time. They can cut watering in half.

- **Mulch your planters.** Adding a ¹/₂-inch or so of mulch helps retain vital moisture on hot days and gives your planting beds a neat appearance.

- **Because frequent watering washes nutrients from the soil,** it's a good idea to fertilize your new plants regularly. When planting, add a slow-release fertilizer. Then give "snacks" with a liquid fertilizer. For flowering plants, choose a bloom booster formula.

- **Pinch off spent blooms and leaves.** Take a few pleasurable moments each day to pinch or trim off spent leaves and flowers. This routine, called "deadheading," actually encourages more growth by redirecting a plant's nutrients toward new blossoms and young leaves.

well as corner stones and capstones for the top course. Be sure to overlap the joints between stones on each successive row. Many landscape blocks are designed to interlock from one course to the next.

5. Check level frequently to make sure that each course of stone is level. If not, adjust the gravel bed as necessary by adding or removing material. After each course is completed, partially backfill the bed. Use excellent quality topsoil, purchased in bulk, for most of the bed.

6. Finish with capstones by securing the top course with landscape adhesive to prevent them from sliding out of place. Allow the adhesive to cure for a day. Then plant!

Color in Your Front Yard

Nothing adds sparkle and life to a landscape like colorful plantings. And you can add any hue of the rainbow in minutes! Here are great ideas for giving your yard colorful curb appeal that will last all growing season.

- **Paint pots.** Clean plastic, clay, metal, or wood containers well and spray paint in a bright, trendy color (such as apple green, citrus yellow, or electric blue). Choose a paint that specifies use for that material.

- **Paint the front door and trim.** Choose a bright color that coordinates with the siding of your house. Include any window boxes or planters.

- **Add fabric.** If you have a bench or chair in your front yard, add a brightly colored cushion or two, made of outdoor fabric resistant to sun and rain.

- **Add an outdoor rug or mat.** Brighten up your front door (and prevent tracked dirt) with a colorful rug or mat made for outdoors. Or get really bold and use exterior paint to paint a ruglike pattern on your front landing.

- **Grow plants where there is no soil.** If you have a dull strip of concrete or bare soil where nothing will grow, add a pot filled with colorful annuals (impatiens are great for shade) right on top of the problem area.

- **Add hanging baskets.** If there's no room for pots, add a hanging basket or two. Hang from porches or the sides of houses, or purchase a shepherd's hook to place alongside a walkway or drive.

- **Don't forget the garages.** The fronts of garages, with their huge expanse of concrete, can look forlorn. Add large pots of drought-tolerant annuals on either side of garage doors. Plant a sprawling vine alongside the edge of the drive to grow on a trellis erected over the doors.

COLORING THE WAY
Framed by a spray of colorful perennials, glazed terra-cotta pots, and a dark green overhanging canopy, this stucco entryway has blossomed into a multihued portal.

A CHEERY GREETING
Set off by their crisp white, two-tiered planter boxes, these pink impatiens add a dazzling show of color to the front of a suburban house.

The Urban Landscape

No room? No problem. Landscape even a tiny brownstone or other tight space fast and inexpensively. Window boxes are the obvious solution. Look for window boxes as wide as the window. Or make ones as wide as the window. Other solutions include:

- **Check out the various types of hardware** that allow you to hang pots on the sides of buildings. Install hooks for hanging baskets.

- **Fill your front step with pots.** Group as many as you can without blocking foot traffic. If you're worried about someone taking them, before planting, run a thin chain through the drainage hole in the pot and secure the pot to a railing or other sturdy anchor.

- **Think vertically.** Plant vines that will cloak a railing or side of your building with color and fragrance. Trellises are inexpensive to buy and easy to mount.

- **Make planter box–type raised beds.** If you have nothing but a stretch of concrete to work with, make simple boxes a few feet wide and long. Drill holes in the bottom for drainage. If they're at least a foot high (preferably 18 inches), you'll be able to grow a wide range of annual flowers and vegetables in them.

Don't be afraid of color. Here, a riot of shades gives this yard a romantic, cottage feel. Climbing roses on the pergola over the front door perfume the air, and a clipped boxwood hedge along the path gives the yard a sense of boundary.

QUICK APPEAL:

All those cute garden accents are fun to look at, but use a measure of caution when adding them to your garden. Garden accents are like jewelry—it's easy to add too much and the result can be overwhelming. Instead, choose just one or two functional garden accents (such as a bench or real birdhouse) for your garden. Then allow yourself one or two fun accents for decoration only, such as an endearing little frog or other sculpture.

Make an Island Garden

An island garden or bed is an attractive way to add definition, texture, and color to a large expanse of lawn. An island garden doesn't have to be large to have a big impact, and 50 to 75 square feet is usually adequate. The garden pictured here features a low wall of limestone block to provide more visual interest. To maximize curb appeal, try designing walls with gentle curves. Remember that perennials will bloom the first summer of planting, but it will take up to three years for them to reach their peak in height and color.

1. Mark out the bed with a garden hose to create pleasing curved edges for the island, adjusting the shape until you're satisfied. Make the edges of the island bed directly on your lawn with spray paint. You might want to check the shape from across the street to see how it will fit into the overall front landscape.

2. Remove grass from the area, using a spade or a sod cutter. You can use this sod elsewhere in your landscape to fill in spots. Otherwise, just dig up the turf and toss it in the compost pile. Use a spade to gently turn over the exposed soil. Add bags of composted manure, regular compost, or sphagnum peat moss. As a rule of thumb, spread 1 to 3 inches of a soil amendment over the surface of the bed.

3. Dig a trench 3 to 4 inches deep as a foundation for the block wall. Fill the trench with gravel and compact the gravel with a hand tamper. Make sure the gravel bed is level.

Working with Limestone Blocks

The limestone used in this project is typically referred to as "planter block." It's good for low walls, edging, and, as the name suggests, small planters. Wall block is similar but larger and heavier, so it's a better choice for taller walls (more than a couple of feet tall). Both types come in sections about 3 feet long and need to be cut to the desired lengths.

You can cut the block with a wet saw or with a masonry blade on a circular saw. The circular saw is noisier and extremely dusty; however, a circular masonry blade costs much less (about $15) than renting a wet saw.

If the saw won't cut through the full thickness of the block, saw a groove on four sides, then tap with a mallet or small sledgehammer to finish the break. The break is usually fairly clean, but you may need to chip off some points with a hammer to create a cleaner face.

Building a limestone wall at the back of a flowerbed adds an attractive backdrop for your plants as well as the character and substance that only natural stone can bring.

4. Lay the block or stone to the desired height. Make sure to overlap the joints between the blocks with each successive row.

5. Position plants next to the planting area to figure spacing. Be sure to place each plant in the soil to the same depth they were growing in the ground or in their pots.

6. Fill in the bed, keeping in mind the size of each plant at maturity. After planting, mulch with 1 to 3 inches of wood chip or other mulch to suppress weeds and conserve moisture. Then water deeply, allowing the water to seep down several inches into the soil. Keep well watered for a week or two until the plants get established.

CHAPTER FOUR

Walkways

THE WALKWAY LEADING TO YOUR FRONT DOOR is more than just a path—it's an invitation to your home. Taken together with your front entrance, a walkway is key to establishing the visual personality of your house. It may be short, but it should be as interesting as it is welcoming. Walkway shape, texture, and color all play a role in ushering friends, family, and visitors to your front door.

The walkway leading to your front entry connects to the sidewalk or street, to an adjacent driveway, or both. It can be curved, meandering, stepped, or straight as an arrow. Whatever the general design, access to your walkway and the front entrance to your house should be readily apparent. The beginning should be clearly visible or indicated by landscape features, such as a gate, arbor, or distinctive shrubbery.

There are very few rules for walkway designs, except that they should be relatively flat, level, and easy to negotiate. Walkways paved with stone or brick should be free of dips and bumps—it's a good idea to check paved walkways annually for any individual paving materials that have come out of alignment and reset them.

In general, straight walkways are compatible with formal settings, but that doesn't mean they can't have personality. Beautiful paving materials, carefully chosen edgings, and symmetrically placed seating areas all convey a fine sense of design.

Curved walkways tend to be more informal, inviting the visitor to meander a bit through plantings and other landscaping features. Even short, curved walkways are visually interesting features that add plenty of character to your front yard.

A flagstone walkway set in concrete leads visitors on a winding tour of an expressive front landscape on the way to the front door of this Portland-area home. The rustic appearance of the flagstone and large accent rocks along the edges add to the informality of the walkway.

Planning Your Walkway

Whether you're planning a new walkway or simply looking to spruce up the one you have, the principles of good curb appeal are basically the same: make your walkway inviting; build personality with color and accessories; and strive for harmony by keeping in mind the whole appearance of your home—don't let one outstanding feature dominate the landscape. Here are some great ways to add curb appeal to walkways:

Create the mood. If you like a casual appearance, then let your walkway relax. Soften edges with creeping plants and let nearby shrubs overhang the path. Informal materials, such as salvaged brick and tumbled stone, are unfussy and fun. Add a distinctive garden ornament or cairn of specially chosen rocks to provide visual focal points.

For a more formal approach, use symmetry. Place identical shrubs, lawn ornaments, and outdoor lighting fixtures opposite each other. Keep shrubs and walkway plantings neatly trimmed and off of walking surfaces.

Define the way. Wide paths—those 48 inches wide or wider—offer an open invitation that's easy to identify. For curved walkways or walks that lead to the front door from the driveway, establish a marker, such as a pair of potted plants or garden ornaments, that clearly defines the beginning of the walkway and says, "Start here!"

Add color. Choose plants and pots that bring complementary colors into the overall scheme and help define the edges of the path. Potted plants work especially well because you can move and rearrange them as the mood strikes, or to add different accents.

Another way to add color is to edge your walkway with a border of colored gravel that contrasts and defines the walking surface. For extra pizzazz, use colored tumbled glass. Tumbled recycled glass granules have smooth, safe edges and come in a variety of sparkling colors.

If you're thinking of installing a concrete walkway, try colored concrete. Dry powdered dyes made especially for concrete will give your walkway subtle hues. If you have an existing concrete walk, color it with stains made specifically for concrete.

> Choose plants and pots that bring complementary colors into the overall scheme to help define the edges of the path.

Between the Pavers— To Grow or Not to Grow

Ground-hugging plants such as creeping thyme and Irish moss fill the spaces between pavers and flagstones with a colorful living outline. These plants tolerate moderate foot traffic and are hardy in most zones. In shady spots try Corsican mint and baby's tears. Space pavers 1 to 2 inches apart, depending on the size of the stones you're using. Brush a mixture of 30 percent potting soil and 70 percent sand between the stones, and plant starts 6 inches apart. Be sure to keep young plants well-watered until they are strong and begin to spread, and keep an eye out for weeds and grass until the ground cover completely fills the spaces between the pavers.

To keep plants from growing between the pavers, put down a layer of landscape fabric before adding a sand base for the paving materials. The fabric allows water to drain through but prevents plants from taking root. If any plants do manage to take hold, their root system will be shallow enough so that they can be easily removed.

CASUAL BEAUTY

A luxurious tumble of ornamental grasses and other border plantings is the perfect complement to this broad walkway of dark grey flagstone. The deliberately unfitted pattern of the stone leaves gaps filled by an assortment of stones.

COTTAGE COMFORT

Flagstone walkways are especially attractive in cottage-like settings. The stones may be loose set in sand fill or permanently installed in concrete. This meandering walkway features a small bench—always a welcoming touch.

A SIMPLE FORMALITY

Brick pavers are durable walkway material that can be used in either formal or casual settings, and they blend with most architectural styles. Set in a straight path and lined with low boxwoods, brick makes a classic, welcoming walkway.

DIVERSE MATERIALS

A mixture of brick, stone, and concrete combines to create this expressive walkway. The broad apron abuts the curb, making an attractive and inviting spot for visitors to access the property from a parked vehicle.

Good to Know: Local walkway codes

Any steps along the walkway should be built according to local codes—a general rule is that risers are 7½ inches tall and treads 10 to 11 inches long. If your codes allow it, a gentler step 5 to 6 inches tall with treads 14 to 17 inches long is well proportioned for steps made of stone and brick. Handrails are usually required for three or more steps.

Mixed-Material Walkways

Although many walkway designs feature the use of a single material, such as concrete or brick, you can add a lot of style and character simply by blending two or more types of materials. One of the most popular methods is to create edgings that line the main walkway material.

- **Brick** makes an attractive edging for many other materials, such as flagstone and concrete. Lay brick at right angles to your walkway for maximum stability.

- **Pebbles** or tumbled stone (as opposed to gravel) can be used to fill spaces between stones or squares of concrete. However, you'll need to plan for a way to contain the loose pebbles so they don't spread into your lawn. Landscape edging or a border of brick works well.

- **Decomposed granite** is a rough-textured sand often used to fill spaces between paving materials. It tends to settle over time and needs periodic refilling.

Bold squares of cut slate set in raised borders of brick make a dramatic walkway leading to this front entry. In this case, the grass is integrated into the design, becoming the "fill" material between each broad platform.

Faux Flagstones

Like the look of this flagstone walkway? Look again—it's all concrete. The grout lines are simply painted on. To re-create this look, choose a tough concrete paint or floor enamel for your grout, and pick a color that approximates grout, such as grey or tan.

CONCRETE AND GRAVEL

Easy-to-make poured rectangles of concrete are solid islands in a pathway of colored gravel. The wet concrete was stamped with a straightedge to produce the decorative grooves.

STONE BLEND

With slabs of flagstone serving as steps and round granite rocks as risers, this set of walkway stairs has the rustic charm of a natural river bed. Concrete mortar keeps everything stable.

LIVING MATERIALS

Not all walkway materials are concrete or stone. Low-growing plants, such as Irish moss and creeping thyme, fill in the spaces between stone pavers and become a "living grout" that adds unique texture to a walkway.

STEPPING STONES

With squares of cut flagstone set in a gravel bed, this narrow, plant-lined side walkway leads visitors through a quiet garden. Landscape fabric placed under the gravel bed keeps plantings from intruding into the walkway.

Concrete pavers are ideal walkway materials. Made especially to withstand foot traffic and climate extremes, concrete pavers come in many sizes, styles, and colors to match any exterior scheme. They are lightweight and have uniform thickness that makes installation an attractive do-it-yourself project. Interlocking varieties create unique patterns and are especially stable.

QUICK APPEAL:

Inspect brick, flagstone, and pavers regularly for broken or loose mortar of paving units. These should be repaired before water and ice do more extensive damage. Areas of your walkway that are consistently shady promote the growth of mildew, which in addition to being unsightly can be dangerously slippery. Remove mildew, moss, and algae by scrubbing the surface with a stiff bristle brush or broom dipped in a 50-50 mix of bleach and water. Avoid splattering the leaves of nearby plants. If plants are at risk, first cover them with a sheet or lightweight plastic tarp.

Paving Your Walkway with Brick and Stone

True, stone costs a good deal and it's hard, heavy, and unyielding. But you can buy native rock from a local stoneyard, which makes stone more affordable than you might think. Remember this, too: Rock is permanent, making a stone or brick paver walkway a sensible financial decision in the long run.

Before you check out the local stone dealer, you should have a rough idea of the size of your walkway in terms of total square feet. A typical walkway is at least 2 feet wide, but a minimum of 40 inches wide is recommended so that two people can approach your entryway walking comfortably side-by-side.

Multiply the width by the total length of your walkway in feet, and add 15 percent for waste and breakage. If you plan curves, measure them by laying out a rope or garden hose in the shape of your proposed walkway. When you've got it right, mark the beginning and end points, straighten out the hose, and measure the marked length.

Quarried stone comes in a variety of sizes and shapes. In fact, almost every stone is available in every shape for landscaping, which means a uniform look can be achieved. Your stone dealer will show you what rock is available for your project, how many tons you'll need, tips on installation, and so on.

Home Delivery

Don't be shy about stopping in and checking out your local stoneyard. Many of them have on-staff professionals happy to provide suggestions on the choice of stone and base underlayment. They'll also check out your site, give advice on drainage, and refer you to qualified contractors if your project is beyond your abilities.

Delivery services are available at all stoneyards for a nominal fee. Don't attempt to load stone in your car—it's not worth the risk of damage to your vehicle or your back. The stone company will deliver the materials directly to you. Many delivery trucks have backhoes that come along for the ride; have the company deliver the materials as close to the actual job site as possible because you don't want to cart rock from the end of the driveway, around the house, and to the backyard.

A LIVING STAIRWAY
A meandering stepped walkway of flagstone leads indirectly—but beautifully—toward the entry of this country-style house. Loose-laid rock walls lining the walkway add to the charm of the entryway garden.

WALKWAY PATH
Large pieces of flagstone form the main surface of this simple path. Although the joints between the stones are large, washed pea-gravel fills the gaps and extends to the edge of the walkway to provide definition. Landscape fabric installed under the stones keeps weeds and grasses at bay.

Flagstone

Durable and attractive flagstones, such as limestone and bluestone, are often used for walkways. They are best set in mortar but can be bedded in sand or crushed rock. Iowa limestone is valued for its consistent color and density. Lannon stone, also known as Wisconsin limestone, has a white-gray appearance and is denser than Iowa limestone. Sandstone comes in the widest range of colors and is considerably softer than limestone, making it very easy to work with.

Bricks and Blocks

Less expensive than flagstone, manufactured materials such as brick and concrete offer value and easy installation, even for the novice landscaper. They are available in many shapes, colors, and sizes at your local stoneyard. If you need to match existing brick, special orders also are possible. Bricks are made of clay, fired in a kiln at 1,900° F, and come in shades of red, brown, and yellow. For hardscaping purposes, bricks you want to know about are:

Building bricks

These bricks can be used for virtually any construction purpose. They come in a standard nominal 8×4-inch size (which means they are actually $7\frac{5}{8} \times 3\frac{5}{8}$ inches in size—the mortar in between the bricks

Good to Know: Be prepared for hauling stone

If possible, rent a backhoe for a day or so if you are installing your stone project yourself. If that's not feasible, make sure you have a heavy-duty, contractor-grade wheelbarrow—a small one will wilt under the weight when hauling a load of rock or brick around the yard. Above all, if you're moving rock around, watch your back.

makes up the difference). They are graded according to their ability to withstand various weather conditions. Grade SW (severe weather) is used in regions that experience severe winters or for projects that come in contact with the ground (such as retaining walls and patios). Grade MW (moderate weather) is used in regions that experience moderate winters; use this grade for aboveground walls but not for patios or retaining walls.

Paving bricks

These bricks are harder than building bricks, come in true 8×4-inch size, and are installed without mortar. They are used for dry-laying in sand for patios, paths, and driveways. They are graded according to how much traffic load they can bear (use type 2 or 3) and how much weather they can stand (use class SX for severe winters or MS for moderate winters).

Concrete paving and retaining wall materials have made great leaps in the past few years; gone are the plain grey versions of the past. Concrete now comes in a multitude of colors and textures suitable for any home landscape. Concrete materials are also the easiest of hardscape items to install. They include:

Patio blocks

Available in modular sizes of 24×24, 12×12, and 12x6 inches, patio blocks may be laid on a bed of sand and are the easiest and fastest way to create a patio. New patterns make these blocks attractive as well as affordable.

Interlocking blocks

Used for retaining walls, interlocking blocks are a mortarless system, making them an ideal choice for the home landscaper to create planting beds and small retaining walls. (For retaining walls higher than 3 or 4 feet, we recommend professional installation to deal with the logistics of retaining that much earth.) Interlocking blocks are available in a wide range of colors. New on the market are tumbled blocks, which tone down the commercial feel.

Man-made materials, such as the paving brick here, look great when paired with natural stone. Because of their uniform shape, pavers make excellent edgings for outlining and defining a flagstone walkway.

Universal Design: Walkways

Making your walkway welcoming and accessible to everyone isn't difficult, but it does require planning. A continuous walkway of smooth concrete is ideal—there should be no steps or bumps to negotiate. The landing area directly in front of the door should be level, at least 5 feet square, and flush with the entry. Thresholds should be no more than $1/2$ inch high.

The recommended slope for a walkway is a 5 percent grade, or no more than one vertical foot of elevation for every 20 feet of walkway. Walkways should be at least 36 inches wide—walkways 48 to 54 inches wide allow two people to walk side-by-side.

Concrete pavers are a good do-it-yourself project. When set in sand, the pavers will have a slightly uneven surface reminiscent of a century-old cobblestone walkway.

Build a Walkway with Paving Stones

Few curb appeal features are as inviting as a thoughtfully designed walkway. In providing access to the front door, a walkway made of brick, stone, and concrete pavers—or a combination of materials—will beautify your landscape and enhance your home's street presence. Placing pavers on a sand base in what's known as a "dry set," you can make an outstanding front walkway in a weekend.

TIP: In areas where moisture may be a problem, sand-set pavers allow water to seep between the cracks rather than divert toward the house. Sand-set pavers are also easy to replace—so save a few after your installation for potential fixes.

1. Mark the walkway. To frame a straight walkway, use string attached to two stakes as a guide. To frame a curved walkway, lay a garden hose as desired. Once the outlines are established, mark the borders directly onto the dirt, grass, or garden area with chalk or spray paint. This allows for

more accurate cuts along the perimeter.

2. Trench the walkway. With a shovel or trenching tool, cut a level trough approximately 6 inches deep along the length of the walkway. Slope the bottom surface of the trench slightly

away from structures to facilitate drainage (approximately 1 inch every 4–8 feet).

3. Add edging. Add an edge restraint designed for pavers and purchased by the length. Install with metal spikes to both sides of the trench to stabilize the

Keeping Up Appearances

Although brick, flagstone, and concrete pavers will last for decades, individual pieces occasionally crack or come loose. If the loose piece has been mortared in place, use a cold chisel to break out the surrounding mortar, then pry the piece out. Vacuum or brush out any loose material from the hole, then reset the piece in mortar using these steps:

1. Add water to ready-mix mortar, available at home improvement centers, until it is the consistency of toothpaste.

2. Spread an inch-thick layer into the hole, then press the brick, flagstone, or concrete paver into the mortar, taking care to level the piece and make it flush with the surrounding pavers. Let the piece set overnight.

3. The next day, use a grout bag to squeeze fresh mortar around the paver, and smooth the mortar with the back of an old spoon.

If the brick, flagstone, or concrete paver was bedded on sand and has sunk below ground level or otherwise become displaced, pry it out with a screwdriver or small pry bar. Add sand to the hole, then press the paver back into place. Adjust the amount of sand as necessary. Sweep sand into the cracks between the pavers to refill any gaps.

MATERIALS AND TOOLS:

- Pavers (see page 48)
- Landscape fabric (optional)
- Gravel (optional base)
- Plastic edging
- Coarse sand
- Fine-grain silicate sand (top coat)
- Top-coat sealer for pavers (optional)
- String and stakes or garden hose
- Chalk or spray paint
- Shovel or trenching tool
- Tamper (hand or electric)
- Metal spikes
- Rake
- Screed (straightedge)
- Masonry saw (optional)
- Safety glasses
- Ear plugs
- Dust mask
- Broom

walkway, preventing drift from weather and foot traffic. The edge also serves as a weed barrier.

4. Partially fill with sand and level.
Depending on the depth of the pavers, fill roughly two-thirds of the trench with coarse sand and rake it smooth.

(One cubic yard of sand provides a 1-inch-thick base for 300 square feet.)

Make a screed or straightedge by screwing a 2×4 to a piece of plywood 3 inches wide and as long as the walkway is wide. Drive a nail into each end of the 2×4 so the distance between the nail

and a plywood edge is equal to the thickness of your pavers. Level the sand by guiding the screed's nails back and forth along the top of the trench. Add sand to low spots, and remove sand that builds up. The sand should be solid but not compacted.

Lighting Your Walkway

Low-voltage lighting is an inexpensive way to add good looks and safety to your walkway. There are styles available to match any scheme—from traditional to modern—and finishes that include brass, copper, brushed aluminum, chrome, and more. During the day, walkway lighting adds a bit of design flair with shapes such as miniature hanging lanterns, flowers, and dramatic tubes. During the night, your walkway will be illuminated with pools of light that are eye-catching from the street and welcoming beacons for those walking up to your front door.

Low-voltage lighting systems are safe and economical. Because the cables carry so little voltage, many of the precautions required for normal electrical wiring are unnecessary, making installation quick and easy. You can choose to put the lights on a timer that will turn the lights on and off according to your specifications, or opt for a light sensor that will turn the lights on at dusk and off at dawn.

Low-voltage outdoor light kits typically include five or more lights, cable, and a transformer/timer. Some lights are mounted on stakes poked into the ground; others can attach to posts. The cable runs in a shallow trench or sits on top of the ground, covered with mulch; the transformer/timer simply plugs into a standard outdoor receptacle.

Good walkway lighting casts a glow downward, toward the walking surface, and shields glare from reaching eyes. With their capped tops, these lantern-type walkway lights perform perfectly.

MULTITASKING

Set in the midst of a walkway planting bed, a series of low-voltage light fixtures illuminate both the walking surface and the surrounding flowers, adding a dash of color even at night.

TEMPORARY LIGHTING

Free-standing, battery-operated luminaries are a great way to temporarily light steps and walkways for special occasions, such as holiday celebrations or Halloween trick-or-treating.

Solar Lighting

Solar walkway lights are wireless and hassle-free. They don't need wires or cords because they generate their own electrical energy by absorbing light energy and storing it in a battery. The newest-generation solar lights utilize the latest LED technology to provide exceptional light quality with minimum power drain on the battery.

Solar lighting costs about the same as traditional low-voltage outdoor lighting. Choose from pendant lanterns; wall-, canopy-, pier-, and post mounts; outdoor table lamps; and outdoor security lights. Solar lights are also found in a variety of decorative finishes capable of matching your home's decor.

Most solar lights have fewer moving parts than traditional lights. Their simple design and construction can make for a longer-lasting product. Plus, solar lighting is completely off the grid! If your neighborhood loses power, your solar-powered system will continue to provide safe, efficient lighting for your walkway.

Solar lighting systems are an easy afternoon project. Depending on your system, all you should need is a screwdriver to assemble a few of the parts. It's a great project to do with children because it's shock-free and safe.

Solar walkway lights should be placed 10 feet apart. Your solar bulbs are capable of outputting as much light as your incandescent bulbs. High-quality solar lighting, placed where it can absorb the full amount of sunlight to fully charge its battery, can offer light for a full 15 hours.

Installing Low-Voltage Walkway Lighting

MATERIALS AND TOOLS:

- Transformer
- Waterproof outlet cover
- Low-voltage cable
- Wire strippers
- Shovel
- Low-voltage light fixtures and bulbs
- Ground stakes

Walkway lighting is a simple do-it-yourself project that has a big impact on your home's curb appeal. In the evening and at night, walkway lighting provides soft illumination that makes negotiating steps and curved walkways easier and safer. During the day, well-designed fixtures add a bit of character to your entryway. You'll find low-voltage walkway lighting fixtures to match any architectural style at home improvement centers and lighting design stores. Be sure to follow the manufacturer's instructions for safe installation.

Low-voltage lighting is a stylish way to add personality and safety to your walkway. Most low-voltage systems can be installed in a day by a homeowner with moderate do-it-yourself skills.

1. Install the transformer. Mount the transformer on a post, stake, or the exterior of your house at least 1 foot above the ground and within 1 foot of a ground fault circuit interrupter (GFCI). If the transformer contains a photocell, make sure this location is not shielded from the sun, and also keep the transformer turned off or unplugged while installing. Apply a waterproof cover over the outlet for added weather protection.

2. Attach the cable. Check the manufacturer's instructions to determine the size (or gauge) of the cable you need. To attach the cable to the transformer, use the wire strippers to remove about $5/8$ to $3/4$ inch of insulation from the cable wires. Then slide the stripped wires under the terminal screws on the bottom of the transformer. The wire should easily glide into the designated slots at the transformer's lower end.

3. Lay the cables and arrange the light fixtures. With the first fixture in your run at least 10 feet from the transformer, determine the placement

Lighting Styles

The popularity of outdoor lighting means fixtures are available in a wide variety of styles, sizes, and finishes. Many of these handsome additions to your yard are low-voltage varieties that are perfect for a do-it-yourself weekend project. Before you start planning, however, here are some pitfalls the first-time installer should try to avoid:

- Don't place too many lights on the walkway, especially when lighting both sides of the path. Known as the "runway effect," too many lights can overwhelm your scheme.

- Avoid excessive brightness by checking the manufacturer's recommendations for proper spacing.

- Don't place lighting where it can shine directly into your neighbor's home.

- Always consider your pathway lighting together with other sources of outdoor lighting, such as porch lighting and landscape lights.

of each light. For even illumination, leave 8 to 10 feet between fixtures.

4. Bury the cables. Bury the cables in a 3- to 6-inch-deep trench, leaving a small amount of slack at each light juncture to connect the fixtures. Leave a small amount of cable sticking out of the soil at each fixture location.

5. Assemble the fixtures. Follow the manufacturer's instructions to attach each light to a cable at each juncture. Most lights attach to a cable with a two-part connector that pierces and locks into place. Turn on the transformer to make sure the connection is successful.

6. Install the fixtures. Attach each fixture to a ground stake. The top of each stake should be flush with the ground. Do a final check at night to make sure that you have the right amount of light and that the fixtures are upright. Then push the cable and connector under the soil about 2 inches.

CHAPTER FIVE

Entryways

ENTRYWAYS ARE REALLY MANY SEPARATE ELEMENTS brought together around the idea of approaching and entering a home. There are walkways, stairs, and front doors, and perhaps a porch as well. Details, such as well-chosen light fixtures and door hardware, all contribute to the magic of the entryway. For great curb appeal, all these components work together to provide a sense of welcome and invitation. Composing these elements and making sure they are all in harmony is one of the most compelling aspects of good curb appeal. Here are great ways to ensure your entryway is a point of pride for your home:

• If you have a roofed entryway, add an outdoor ceiling fixture or a pair of coach lanterns. Use that extra illumination to make your house numbers more visible by placing them inside the entry area.

• Providing built-in seating, chairs, or a bench near your entry is a hospitable touch that says you're willing to sit and chat with neighbors, or converse with door-to-door solicitors without letting them past the front door.

• Add a built-in mail slot in the wall next to the front door so that mail won't pile up outside when you're away for several days.

• The door handle is the first thing many visitors will touch, so invest in a high-quality lockset that gives a solid first impression when you invite guests inside.

• If you want to shelter your front entry but a porch is not appropriate or practical, add a portico. A portico is a simple, small roof, usually supported by a pair of posts, that protects your front door from the elements. A portico not only provides cover, but also gives your entry more visual interest and curb appeal.

A brick walkway, entryway gardens, and a welcoming porch set with pots of flowers and a bold American flag provides a grand entrance to this charming turn-of-the-century home.

Elements of Great Front Entries

CONTEMPORARY CURVE

Add visual interest to your entryway with an attention-getting walkway. Although not a true curve, these architecturally designed steps have a meandering appearance. Build walkways that are 42 to 48 inches wide so two people can walk side-by-side.

A WELCOME SIGHT

A boldly colored front door in a contrasting color is a traditional way to indicate the main entry of a house. Friendly brick steps and a sheltering portico with a curved ceiling frame this door and create an impressive entryway.

SPLASHES OF COLOR

This simple entryway has a strong presence with its arched doorway and a front door painted a bright contrasting color that complements the stone façade. Cheery arrangements of plants in matching blue pots add splashes of color and frame the front steps.

BY THE NUMBERS

Architectural details, such as decorative brackets, moldings, columns, and trim, give your house a dash of personality. The stylized oversize house numbers are actually cutouts carefully incised into the board trim, and are easily seen from the street.

BOLD PORTICO

This carefully orchestrated entryway has all the right ingredients: a contrasting front door, an architecturally interesting portico with a decorative window, good lighting, and landscaping that blends well with the classic lines of the structural components.

GRAND ENTRY

Pairs of portico columns and double doors make everything twice as nice on this impressive portico entry. The extra-wide walkway with its stone curb sweeps visitors toward the front door with a grand gesture.

POINTING THE WAY

Although a porch roof runs the length of this house, the entryway is indicated by its own front-facing gable roof. This additional little roof is architectural language that says, "The front door is right here!"

STYLE HARMONY

Keeping entryway elements in the same design "family" helps establish architectural harmony. Choose the same color or type of finish for exterior elements such as entrance hardware, door knockers, house numbers, mailboxes, and porch lights.

USE SIMILAR MATERIALS

Changing exterior materials is one way to emphasize the importance of the front door. Here, an expressive front door with a round-top window is framed by a fieldstone veneer that contrasts with the shingle siding on the rest of the house. Notice how the fieldstone is repeated on the steps, harmonizing the elements of the entry.

REPEAT ELEMENTS

Adding generous amounts of glass around your entry door brings lots of light into the interior, but has the effect of opening up the exterior or your house as well. Glass signals that your house is an open, friendly place. Window grids provide visual texture.

Creating Symmetry

Symmetry is an easy way to add curb appeal to an entry. By repeating key elements on either side of a central point of focus—in this case, the front door—you'll build a sense of balance and proportion that's pleasing to the eye and simple to arrange. Symmetrical compositions of light fixtures, twin arrangements of potted plants, and front-door accents are classic ways to create welcoming entryways. Adding identical sidelights with accent-colored trim greatly enhances the effect.

Universal Design: Entryways

1. Make sure the main entrance and at least one other exterior passage are accessible to everyone. They should have no steps and thresholds that are no more than $\frac{1}{2}$ inch high along their entire length.

2. Entering with packages and other items can be difficult, so include a covered entry and provide a shelf or bench both inside and outside the door. Provide a clear, level space on both sides of the door.

3. A motion detector can ensure that the entry is lighted when you arrive home. For convenience and peace of mind, install a home-automation system, including an intercom system that is linked to the front entry.

4. Equip the entry door and other doors with easy-to-use levers instead of knobs. Electronic locksets can replace keys for entry doors.

Creating an Entryway Garden

Few entryway elements are as pretty as a well-planned garden. An entryway garden doesn't have to be big and bold—a few well-chosen perennial plants will create a living entry that is easy to take care of and that looks good in all four seasons. Long-blooming perennials like coreopsis, daylily, and scabiosa provide color from spring through fall, as well as attractive foliage when not in bloom. Maidengrass and yew provide color and texture into the winter, even when the perennials are asleep under the snow.

Before you begin planting, check your soil for a good, crumbly texture that should remind you of chocolate cake. If you squeeze a little in your hand, it sticks together somewhat but still crumbles apart easily. If you think you need to improve your soil quality, try these simple remedies for various types of soil conditions:

Clay soil: Add organic matter—compost, composted manure, peat moss, and humus—and turn the soil with a garden fork or spade to a depth of 4–6 inches. Don't add only sand to heavy, compacted clay soils or you'll risk creating a concrete-like substance. Mix sand with peat moss or compost first and then thoroughly mix into soil. Add organic matter annually until soil is the desired consistency.

Sandy or high-silt soil: Blend topsoil with compost or peat moss and add to soil.

Alkaline soil: Mix peat moss or oak leaf mold into planting beds to lower the pH. Some plants, such as azaleas, rhododendrons, camellias, and blueberries, need acidic soil.

ABOVE: Precise, rectangular beds edged in brick give this entry garden a sense of formality. LEFT: Loosely piled river rock is the perfect complement to the untamed look of this casual cottage entry garden. RIGHT: Placed exactly in front of the entryway steps, this formal little garden gains added importance. A pedestal birdbath calls attention to the lush plantings.

Making an Entryway Arbor

Arbors are perfect for framing a pretty view or dressing up a path. They act as portals to your property, and their design is perfect for encouraging a canopy of climbing plants to cover the top with flowers and greenery. This one serves all purposes admirably, and it's easy to make in a weekend. You'll need a fairly well equipped toolbox to bring it to life, including a circular saw or a small handsaw and miter box for making precise cuts.

After your arbor is built and installed, and you're ready to plant, choose vines known for their climbing ability, such as annual morning glory, cypress vine, or thunbergia, for easy color from seed that lingers until frost. Compost annual vines after frost knocks them down.

1. Choose the wood. Build the arbor from rot-resistant wood. Cedar and redwood are excellent choices for minimal maintenance, and both weather beautifully. You also can use pressure-treated pine or fir, though you'll have to check carefully for warped pieces when purchasing the wood.

2. Dig holes. Measure placement of the four main 2×4 posts, and dig four holes 18 inches deep. Fill with 6 inches of gravel to provide drainage around the posts.

3. Cut lumber to length. The upright posts (A) come in 8-foot lengths and do not need to be cut. Cut the four 1×4 top rails (B) into 7-foot-3-inch lengths. If you wish to add the optional 1-inch-diameter decorative hole, use the following trick: Before cutting a rail to length, draw a line with a pencil where the 30-degree cut and optional decorative hole will go. Mark and drill the hole in the proper location with a 1-inch flat bit, then cut off the end along your marked line.

4. Cut spindles. If you did not purchase precut deck spindles, cut the thirteen 2×2s (C) to 3 feet 6 inches each using a 45-degree bevel on both ends. (We beveled 2×2s in the arbor shown in the photograph. The arbor in the illustration is shown with precut spindles, sometimes called deck spindles, which are already cut and beveled.) Cut the common lath (D) into 24 pieces of 3 feet each.

5. Assemble the sides. There are a number of ways to assemble the trellis, but the easiest is to take the four uprights (A) and lay them on their narrow sides on a flat surface and with the ends flush. Push them together side by side. Using a square and pencil, measure and mark the location of the lattice (as indicated in the illustration) on all four sides facing up.

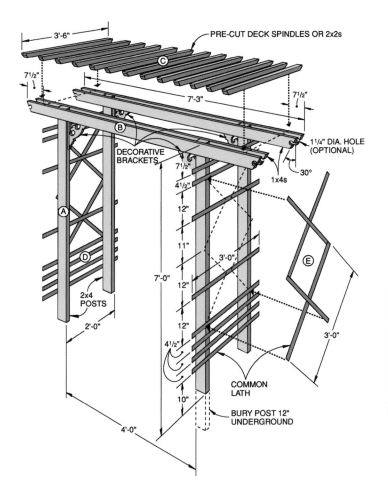

Sprightly and colorful morning glories are a favorite vining plant that presents a continual show of perky flowers. Annual varieties must be planted anew each spring.

Assemble the sides of the arbor by laying two of the upright post pieces on the ground exactly 2 feet apart at their outside edges. Then nail on the lath pieces almost the way you would construct a ladder. (For durability, use construction adhesive at all joints.) Making sure the frame remains square and properly spaced during assembly, nail the bottom lath piece and then the top lath piece. Continue with the remaining six pieces of horizontal lath for that side of the arbor. Tip: If the lattice cracks, predrill holes before nailing.

After the horizontal lattice is installed, nail on the diagonal pieces (E). Repeat the process to assemble the other side of the arbor.

Set the two assembled ends into the holes, keeping them level, square, and properly spaced. Tip: Temporarily tack two 2×2s or other pieces of wood across the bottom of the trellis front and back to keep everything square. Fill hole with soil, and tamp well with your foot.

6. Assemble the top. Lay the four top rails so narrow sides face up. Using the square, measure and mark the spacing (4½ inches apart) for the 13 top pieces (C).

Install the marked top rails (B) using three 2-inch screws per joint. Check for square. Using the marks on the top of the top rails, install the top 2×2s (C) with 3-inch screws. Tip: For easier installation, predrill holes in just one of the 2×2s, then use it to measure and mark the holes on the remaining 2×2s. If using, screw in the optional decorative brackets with 1-inch screws; fill holes with the manufacturer's wooden plugs.

7. Finish. Give the arbor a coat of white exterior stain as we did, or let it weather. To paint, first coat with primer followed by exterior latex.

CHAPTER SIX

Porches & Porticos

THE PORCH IS AS AMERICAN AS APPLE PIE. During their heyday in the early 20th century (when walking was a popular—and necessary—mode of transportation), porches appeared on most styles of American houses as a way for people to connect with friends and passersby. Today, front-facing porches are returning to fashion. Open to the air yet providing shelter from the elements, a porch is a naturally friendly feature that invites visitors to your front door and provides a transition to the inside of your house. If you're fortunate enough to have a porch—or its smaller counterpart, a portico—you'll want to make it as beautiful and welcoming as possible, with perhaps space and seating for you, your family, and your company.

Fortunately, it doesn't take a lot of effort (or money) to dress up a porch and make it a point of pride for your house. Small details, such as potted plants along the front steps, a seasonal wreath at the front door, and perhaps some architectural detailing for posts and railings, are easy ways to pretty-up your porch. If you have the room, a few weatherproof wicker chairs dressed up with indoor/outdoor fabrics and paired with matching side tables are all you'll need to transform your porch into the sweetest room in the house.

Simple conveniences, such as good lighting, a ceiling fan, and perhaps an electrical outlet so you can listen to music or work on your laptop computer, expand your living area and make your porch a comfortable, enjoyable environment.

Be sure to keep your porch in good repair. Paint or refinish posts and railings frequently, and touch up any peeling or bare spots. Keep your floors protected with durable floor paints or finishes, and check often for any signs of rot or damage. Make sure railings and balusters are sturdy and reliably strong.

With its pots of bright red flowers, pretty hanging light fixture, and welcoming rocking chair, this porch is classic Americana. Painting the porch ceiling a crisp white matches the house trim and ensures that the covered area stays light and bright.

AGELESS APPEAL
With its wide, corner-to-corner porch and jaunty, front-facing gable, this late-19th-century house seems to be all smiles. Although the house itself is modest in size, the expansive porch gives a sense of spaciousness. A leafy hanging plant is a friendly touch.

A Portfolio of Porches & Porticos

Porches have many configurations, from simple porticos that shelter only the front door to magnificent wraparound porches that connect to several interior rooms, have multiple seating areas, and provide generous amounts of extra living space. No matter their size, all porches benefit from a sense of style and personality. That's because they are readily visible to anyone who comes past your home, and they play a key role in establishing curb appeal for your property. Notice that small touches can make a big difference: a flag holder for showing your colors, well-tended plants, and eye-pleasing color combinations enhance even the smallest portico.

A TOUCH OF DRAMA
Adding expressive, slightly oversize posts was all this porch needed to be transformed from simple to simply amazing. Keeping the color scheme neutral only adds to the dramatic architectural flair.

AN AMERICAN CLASSIC
A true American classic, this big, curved, wraparound porch is a signature of farmhouse Victorian style that was popular more than a century ago. Pole lamps and framed artwork on the walls give this porch an especially homey feel.

SMALL SIZE, BIG STYLE
Though diminutive in size, this portico has big style. An arched, "eyebrow-style" roof supported by fanciful columns, stone steps, and symmetrically arranged flower pots gives this entryway both fanciful whimsy and formal dignity.

THE PORCH GOES MODERN
Porches aren't only for classic older homes; modern houses look great with them, too. This distinctive contemporary home features a porch with a lattice screen that creates a private nook at one corner.

PRETTY PLANTINGS
Framed by lush plantings, this straightforward porch is a study in serenity. A white-on-white scheme, accented by square, unadorned posts, gives the porch a quiet strength. A small grouping of white table and chairs welcomes visitors.

Dressing Up–Ideas for Pretty Porches

With a little planning and a day or two's time, you can readily convert a plain porch into an inviting alfresco living room. Wide open to neighborhood sights and sounds, your porch can be a signature statement of your personal style as it makes a major contribution to the curb appeal of your home. Best of all, you'll gain valuable living space that serves as a room to relax and converse, an informal dining area, or simply the best spot in the world to watch the world go by.

While outdoor chairs, tables, and accessories easily can cost as much as any indoor arrangement, a porch is the perfect place to put your imagination to work with inexpensive furnishings, quick-and-easy fabric treatments, and everyday stuff from the house, yard, and garage. Here are some tips to inspire your own porch rejuvenation.

Choose natural textures to keep the focus on the outdoors. Sisal, jute, wicker, rattan, and bamboo are all natural materials that look great in an outdoor environment. Find oversize rustic baskets to hold plants, table linens, or comfy blankets.

Add interest underfoot. Lay down a jute, sisal, or braided rug or a painted canvas floorcloth to warm up and perk up a cement or wood floor. Or paint or stencil the floor with a sturdy floor paint that's suitable for outdoor use.

Blur the line between indoors and out. Place a timeworn table near a window or porch rail and pack it with plants. Use moss-covered concrete garden ornaments, such as statues, urns, and wall plaques, to decorate the space. Bring in a birdbath to hold magazines and seed catalogs, or top it with a piece of glass to make a side table.

Use enough coffee tables and end tables so that every seated person has a place to rest a drink. Also consider using table alternatives, such as benches, crates, or trunks.

Use fabric to visually soften the space. In addition to cushions and seats, use fabric to cover tables, create a privacy screen, or make porch curtains. Durable fabrics for a covered porch include sheeting, ticking, and toweling.

Synthetic, weather-resistant fabrics include woven vinyl-coated polyester and acrylics (available at tent, awning, and fabric stores) that sew easily and are ideal for making soft furnishings and curtains. They dry quickly, don't mildew, and look and feel like indoor fabrics. Also look for laminated-cotton yard goods at the fabric store.

Accessorize with little personal touches that really make a room inviting. Hang birdcages, pictures, mirrors, and collectibles on your exterior walls. For tabletops, think of using lamps, framed photographs, watering cans, birdhouses, and garden statuary.

TIMELESS WICKER
White wicker furniture is an all-time porch favorite. It's both casual and dressy, and works well with most styles of houses. Older wicker can be painted to look like new; the best synthetic wicker is completely weatherproof and looks like real wicker.

ROMANTIC PORCH SWINGS
If you have enough space, consider a porch swing. They're definitely old-school romantic, but this modern daybed version has been given a contemporary touch with vibrant colors accented by a swarm of fanciful pillows and a hanging lamp with a sleek complementary lampshade.

Cheery indoor/outdoor carpet squares are a colorful match for this lively porch grouping featuring stylized synthetic wicker that's weather-resistant. Clouds of flowers in hanging baskets add natural charm.

PAINTED FLOOR
Tough acrylic floor paint is perfect for finishing wood porch floors. Here, the black color harmonizes with the house shutters and presents a neutral base for a simple grouping of natural wicker furniture. A hanging bamboo screen at one end of the porch provides privacy.

PERSONALITY IN PAIRS
Two black wicker rocking chairs furnished with colorful cushions are all that's needed to give this all-white entryway plenty of personality and curb appeal that are readily apparent from the street.

HAPPY COLORS
Bright red wicker furniture, including a hanging porch swing, fills this screened-in porch with happy color. Simple paper globes contribute to the cheeriness.

Seasonal Porch Decorating

Porch decorating doesn't have to be static; you can change it to suit the seasons, holidays, and your mood. Use ready-to-hang fabrics, flags, and simple accessories to give your porch showstopping curb appeal.

The owners of this house made their porch into a Yankee Doodle celebration for the Fourth of July by draping easy-to-make bunting over the railings. Patriotic borders and flag motifs come in a variety of sizes and are readily available at discount stores and home improvement centers. Fabrics for bunting are sold by the yard, so just choose a design in the scale that best fits your project.

1. Measure and cut the amount you need, cut away excess fabric along the scalloped edge, and finish the edge by serging it (or sew a row of stay-stitching along the edge).

2. Hang the fabric from your porch railing, along the roofline, or under each window, attaching it with thumbtacks or duct tape. Printed bunting fabric is realistically shaded and it will look as though draped bunting is fluttering in the wind, even when the yardage is tightly stretched.

This coco fiber basket is an attractive hanging planter all by itself, or place it inside an inexpensive wicker basket as shown on the next page.

Hanging Basket Project

A hanging basket for your front porch is a great way to add color and texture to your décor. Hanging baskets also help blur the distinction between indoors and out, making your porch a living environment.

Although you can buy preplanted hanging baskets at garden centers, you can save money and make your own custom color arrangements with this simple yet satisfying project that can be completed in an hour or so. A coco fiber basket makes an attractive home for the assortment of plants shown here, which include portulaca, coleus, loosestrife, and bracteantha.

Good to Know: Watering wand magic

Hanging baskets are especially prone to evaporation, so diligent watering is important. One of the best types of watering tools is a watering wand, which has a shower-type head on a three-foot-long pole. A finger-operated on/off trigger lets you water easily without creating a mess on your front porch. Some watering wand models include a telescoping extension for watering hard-to-reach baskets and containers.

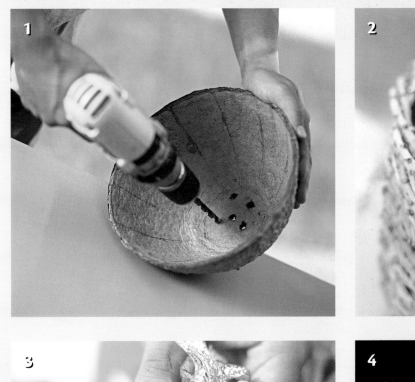

1. Choose your basket. Typical hanging baskets are made of wire or plastic and come in diameters of 8 to 24 inches. Wire basket liners include sphagnum moss, coco fiber, plastic, and pressed paperboard. Sphagnum moss and coco fiber are porous, so they will dry out more quickly than pressed paperboard or plastic; however, the softer materials make it possible to poke planting holes around the outside of the basket. If you use a paperboard liner, drill drainage holes in the bottom before planting.

2. Add soil. Fill the basket with a lightweight potting mix. You can buy a packaged mix or make your own with equal parts peat moss, perlite, and vermiculite. Some prepackaged mixes contain slow-release fertilizer, allowing you to forgo semiweekly treatments with a quick-acting, water-soluble fertilizer. Mix in water-absorbing crystals or line the container with a water-absorbing mat to maintain moisture. Fill the soil to within an inch or two of the rim for ease in watering.

3. Plant the basket. Baskets packed with a single kind of flower have loads of impact. Combinations can be handsome, too, if there's space for the multitude. When using multiple species, include tall, midrange, and trailing forms for variety. Place taller plants near the center and trailing plants along the edges. Try to include varying bloom sizes. For example, vinca, miniature rose, and petunia offer large flowers, while hyssop, lobelia, and calibrachoa have dainty blooms.

4. Water thoroughly after planting. You may have to water daily in hot weather. Lifting a basket is a quick way to judge if it needs water. The lighter the basket, the drier the soil. If the basket dries out during the season, the top of the soil may crust over. Break open the crust and rewet the soil ball thoroughly. Pinch the tops of plants if they begin to look leggy.

Railings & Architectural Details

Porches feature exposed structural members, such as posts, pillars, and brackets, and raised porches have railings and balusters. These key architectural elements present many opportunities for adding special details and flourishes that will give your porch exceptional charm and character.

If it's time to replace any structural parts, be sure to look online for suppliers of porch systems. Most manufacturers feature an array of options to fit any style of house. Although wood is a traditional porch material, parts made from vinyl, fiberglass, and composite materials are strong, resist rot, and are virtually maintenance-free. You can mix materials, too. Topping off your existing wooden porch posts with fiberglass finials is an easy way to add style.

VINYL SYSTEM
Railing systems made of durable vinyl feature everything you need for great style: posts, finials, railings, and decorative balusters. While colors are limited for vinyl products, the material never needs repainting and is impervious to rot.

ADDING BRACKETS
This arch-top portico has been given an extra dash of style with a decorative bracket. Weather-resistant brackets made of fiberglass and composite materials can be attached easily with simple tools.

CRAFTSMAN LOOK

Square, Craftsman-style pillars set on stone pedestals make an eye-catching statement on this architecturally modest split-level suburban house. Artificial stone cladding is an easy way to add the look of stone at a fraction of the cost.

CUSTOM RAILING

Although this entryway is simple, it makes the most of its opportunity for curb appeal with a stone-clad entry and a beautiful, custom-made wrought iron railing. Having the steps and railing curve toward the front door is an added artistic touch.

STOCK COLUMNS

A porch entryway flanked by classic tapered columns is the picture of quiet elegance. Columns such as these are available in wood, fiberglass, and composite materials.

CHAPTER SEVEN

Front Doors

FIRST IMPRESSIONS COUNT. That's why front doors play such a critical role in welcoming visitors to your home. The right entry door will add style, grace, and beauty, while increasing your home's value.

Most residential exterior doors are made from wood, wood composites, fiberglass, and steel. Though all are manufactured for the same task, each material has its strong points. To make the best choice for your home, you'll need to evaluate your needs and preferences in such areas as visual appeal, security, insulating properties, maintenance, and budget. Information in the pages ahead will help you with your decision.

As you shop, keep in mind that you are purchasing an entry system, not just a door. Materials used to build the door are important, but so are the effectiveness of the air seal around the door to stop drafts, the strength and ease of use of the lock, the quality of any glass, and other factors. The best door will satisfy all your needs and look great doing it.

While important to composing a welcoming entry, the door itself is just one element in the overall entry design. It's critical how the door interacts with the other pieces that make up the entry. Where appropriate, surround the door with elements such as smartly fashioned trim, elegant sidelights, and complementary exterior lighting. Work with a designer or architect who can give the entire setting a sense of style and balance.

The simple style of this wood entry door is an appropriate complement to the home's Arts and Crafts architecture. With its raised panels, small windows, and an oversize handle, the door fits the style, which emphasizes craftsmanship over ornamentation. Sidelights allow sunlight inside, and the slightly tapered white side trim sets the door apart from the rest of the façade. Lanterns on either side of the door complete the look.

Shopping for Doors

Wood is a good—though not perfect—material for exterior doors. Most wood will warp, crack, and rot as it is exposed to rain and high humidity. Starting with always popular solid-wood panel doors, here are the common choices that have been developed over the last few decades:

- **Wood-panel doors** are constructed from an assembly of interlocking pieces designed to minimize warping. There are usually six panels inserted into a frame. Solid wood has good strength and insulating properties. Hardwoods such as oak are very resistant to denting. All exterior doors must be protected with paint or finish. Any door covered by a porch roof and/or enclosed by a storm door should last much longer than a fully exposed front door.

- **Solid-core flush exterior doors** are constructed with wood frames that surround particleboard cores. The outer surface is usually a veneer glued to the core. Particleboard is quite heavy, which helps block sound. However, solid-core is not generally as durable as other exterior doors.

If not kept protected with paint, the veneer may delaminate from the particleboard. And if the particleboard gets wet, the door can become unusable.

- **Stave-core exterior doors** (also called "core-block doors") look like standard wood-panel doors, and have cores made from thin pieces of wood laminated together. The laminated core is then covered with a wood veneer. This method makes for an extremely stable door. However, the veneer is liable to peel if the door is not finished.

- **Fiberglass exterior doors** are easily molded into most shapes and styles. Fiberglass is durable, hard, and not prone to shrinking, expanding, or warping. These doors are available in a variety of colors and are easy to paint.

- **Steel exterior doors** often have a steel face and an insulating foam core. Others have the foam core but the exterior layer is a wood veneer. The result is a door with good insulating properties that is also very strong and burglar-resistant.

Wood Doors

PROS:
- Unique look of a natural wood species
- Can be purchased as door only and trimmed to fit existing jambs
- Historically authentic for older homes
- Accept paint or stain

CONS:
- Require periodic refinishing
- Severe weathering can cause wood to split or glue joints to fail
- Changes in humidity can cause shrinking, swelling, or warping
- Low insulating value

PRICE:
- $100 for economy grade at a home center
- $750 for better-grade fir, oak, or mahogany
- Up to $12,000 for door system with sidelights, transoms, etc.

A custom wood cathedral-arch door made from knotty alder calls to mind the grace of an English Tudor castle. One beauty of wood is that it is readily shaped into whatever silhouette is desired.

This rustic wooden door would be at home nestled at the front of a Tuscan-style farmhouse or simple cottage. With time, a door of this quality will only gain in value and will be cherished by the owner.

Fiberglass Doors

PROS:
- Look like wood without risk of warping, and won't rust
- Hold paints and gel stains well
- Lightweight
- Polyurethane foam core has high insulating value (up to R-15)

CONS:
- Slightly higher cost than wood or steel
- Can't be trimmed to fit irregular door openings
- Some inexpensive versions are susceptible to cold-weather cracking or core rot

PRICE:
- $275–$600 for basic six-panel door system
- Up to $8,000 for high-end versions with sidelights, transoms, etc.

Like a chameleon, this fiberglass door mimics the natural beauty of wood with its cherry finish. Outer skins on both sides of the door take finish well and can be ordered with wood graining for authenticity.

Beveled and textured glass gleams on this richly figured fiberglass door. Duplicating this look in other materials could match the look, but you would have a hard time re-creating this level of quality.

Steel Doors

PROS:
- Dimensionally stable
- Hold paint well
- Foam core has good insulating value
- Fire-resistant and low-maintenance

CONS:
- Steel skin can rust or dent from impact
- Can't be trimmed to fit irregular door openings
- May perform poorly if not well insulated

PRICE:
- $150–$250 for basic door system
- Up to $7,000 or more for systems with sidelights, transoms, etc.

Two rectangular glass insets and a rich hunter-green finish make this steel door perfect for a traditional home. Paired with sidelights, this level of elegance and security is rare.

This steel door with molded accents arrives ready to paint, so you can choose the right color to complement your home's exterior. When insulated, a steel door muffles sound and helps increase energy efficiency.

Beefing Up Your Security

No one wants a door that doesn't provide any security for the household. The first step in evaluating an entry door's strength is determining its composition. If it's a hollow-core door, replace it; hollow-core doors are just too easy to break through. Also consider replacing a solid wood door if it's not at least 1¾ inches thick, if it's an older door that's seen better days, or if it has loose panels, which will break if kicked. Better door choices are:

Metal-clad doors. These consist of a steel exterior—plain or embossed to resemble wood—attached to a solid wood frame and a fiber core. These are the most secure replacement doors you can buy.

Solid-core wood doors. Newer wood doors combine the security of a reinforced solid core with the good looks of wood panels. These doors are the best way to get protection plus the beauty of wood.

Once all your entry doors pass muster, also consider outfitting your bedrooms with solid-core doors and deadbolt locks. (Or, if there's a single door that separates the living area from your bedrooms, beef up only that door.) It's one more barrier for an intruder, if someone breaks in during the night.

Because security was a concern for this entry, the homeowners installed a steel door. For even more strength, reinforce the frame with steel and purchase a lockset rated Grade 1 for security by the American National Standards Institute.

Value at the Door

An appealing upgrade to your front entry will do more than just lift your spirits every time you walk up to your home or make visitors feel welcome. A fresher, more impressive design can also put money in your pocket should you sell your home. Enhanced entries add as much as 6.6 percent to a home's perceived value, according to a study commissioned by Therma-Tru Doors and conducted by NFO WorldGroup.

In the online study, one group of people looked at images of three homes with common six-panel exterior doors, while another group viewed images of homes with enhanced entries featuring door treatments with decorative glass, sidelights, and transoms. The enhanced styles seen by the second group boosted the perceived value of each home—sometimes by as much as five times the cost of the entry system.

Realtor Diane Lucas of Auburn, Washington, says that she regularly sees what a difference an entry upgrade can make. "Agents and buyers spend several minutes outside the front door when they arrive," Lucas says. "Since most purchasing decisions begin before a buyer even steps into the house, a beautiful, well-tended front door sets the stage for a successful showing—and ultimately, a sale."

In addition to the added visual appeal, a new exterior door can also contribute significantly to stopping air leakage from a home and also offer much higher insulation than an older door. The savings are so significant that federal tax credits, as well as state and local credits, may be available to help cover costs.

This California home features classic Spanish colonial architecture, but it is the bright and inviting front door that immediately draws the eye.

Get a Grip on Hardware

Latches, knobs, hinges, and other hardware pieces are the jewelry for your entry door and help make a statement visitors are sure to remember. Be sure to pick finishes that you appreciate and that blend well with the architectural style of your house. Traditional shiny brass has classic, timeless good looks. Carefully designed and executed dark metal in Arts and Crafts style adds an artistic flair to your entryway. Brushed nickel has a contemporary feel that blends well with the crisp architectural lines of modern homes and houses with International and midcentury design features.

Note that today's hardware manufacturers present an enormous variety of front door hardware in an array of styles and finishes. The best hardware can range in price from $100 to several hundred dollars, so be sure to shop carefully and examine many options before making a final decision. A quality piece of hardware is made to last a lifetime, and you'll want your decision to satisfy your design sensibilities for years to come.

DOOR DRESSING

No matter what style your home is, dress up your entry with a door lockset that complements it. Choose from classic polished brass with a swan-neck handle, rustic burnished brass, or brushed steel with a braid-design handle.

ELEGANT HANDLES

Own a door that deserves a solid-brass door set with such rich character? Ornamental detailing makes this design seem like a visitor from another time.

SMOOTH CONTEMPORARY

Make a statement with this unadorned tubular entry door handleset in nickel. In addition to being attractive, lever-style handles can be used in universal-design settings where a round doorknob is unacceptable.

CIRCULAR STYLE
Worked to appear as old as the hills, this copper door knocker will give guests pause at your front door. Does your visitor want to knock with this piece? Or should it just be admired in silence, as if at an art show?

FUNCTIONAL DESIGN
This traditional door set can be operated with a key, just as most locks are. Or, those who enter can punch a code into the keypad and enter without having to fumble for the key.

Fingerprint Security Lock

What kind of a front-door lock would James Bond have? A biometric, keyless lock, of course. Instead of a key or keypad, biometric locks open with just a swipe of a finger. If the device's electronic scanner confirms that your fingerprint is in its memory, you're in. However, it will never open the door for someone whose fingerprints are not on the list.

Though these battery-powered locks are on the market, they haven't quite yet entered the mainstream. A major consumer lock company manufactured a biometric lock for a couple of years, but reliability problems surfaced and production stopped. Today, several smaller security companies are making these locks for home use and selling them online and through home security companies. Prices start at under $200. Deadbolt locks and full handlesets are available.

Manufacturers say the locks are commercial-grade and solid enough to resist bumping, drilling, or picking. Device memories hold about 50 users and it is easy to add and delete fingerprints, which takes care of letting such people as best friends, maids, and painters into the house when you want. Entrance times can be set, so a day worker may only be allowed into your house Tuesdays between 9 a.m. and 10 a.m., if you choose.

$242 Front Entry Makeover

1. Outdoor Lighting Fixture

A front-door lighting fixture should be bright enough to illuminate the path for visitors, but not so strong that the light is blinding. For added security, purchase a light with a motion sensor, so the light will come on as visitors approach.

2. House Numbers

House numbers can be found in hundreds of styles, from mass-produced numerals to pieces of custom artwork. If the numbers are not illuminated or highly reflective, mount them near enough to your entry light so they can be read at night.

3. Mailbox

Mailboxes come in a myriad of shapes, sizes, colors, and styles. Hanging the mailbox near the front door is convenient, and it adds another visual element if you select one with an appealing shape.

4. Door Knockers

Door knockers can be as simple as a smooth loop of polished brass to an ornate cast lion's head with a knocker attached. Some are traditional, some are playful.

5. Door Handles

Distinguish your home with a handleset that has character. Whether it is a traditional handle with plenty of heft or a smooth contemporary that feels light in the hand, the handle style should reflect your home's style.

Tips for Painting a Door

If your front door's finish has seen better days, take heart. Refinishing a door is a task most do-it-yourselfers can take on and achieve good results. If you are painting the door yourself, you'll want to paint it after all trim and other paintwork in the entry area is complete.

- Leave the door on its hinges for painting, though you will need to remove the door handleset and any other hardware. Clean any dirt or grime from the door with a detergent and let dry. Also, clean hinges with rubbing alcohol.

- Before painting the door itself, start with the frame. Begin painting up from the hinge-side frame bottom to the header and down the striker side.

- For a flat door, start on the hinge-side edge, painting around the door in one direction.

- Using a 4-inch foam roller, run two or three roller widths up the door face, the height of the door. Follow up with a lightly loaded brush, moving from top to bottom. Flow all the paint in one direction to minimize brushstrokes. The finish will be smooth and even.

- If you are working on a panel door, use the roller and brush method as above. Paint each panel, starting with the upper-left panel, going from top to bottom. Next, paint the center vertical stile, rolling and then brushing out the paint. Go back to the top and paint each horizontal rail with roller and brush. Finish up with the outer stiles and edges.

- Allow the paint to dry, following instructions on the paint can. Lightly sand the door and apply a second coat.

More Appealing Makeovers

With just a few elements—paint, house numbers, door handles, door knockers, mailboxes, and light fixtures—you can turn your front door into a warm invitation and a reflection of your personality. A front-door makeover is an easy and expressive way to add curb appeal to your home.

With a little planning and advance shopping, you can complete your makeover in a weekend. The biggest job is painting your front door. The best method is to remove the door entirely, and then remove all hinges, door knockers, and passage locksets prior to painting. Paint the door and let it dry thoroughly before reinstalling it.

Removing the hardware is the perfect opportunity to replace it with updated versions in new colors and styles. Select complementary or matching styles for your mailbox, mail slot, and sconce lighting. When replacing sconces, be sure to first turn off the electricity at your electrical panel. Don't forget the add-ons—planters and door mats add style quickly and inexpensively.

A brilliant blue door outlined with sharp black trim makes an eye-catching portal to your home. Crisp white house numbers and sunny yellow sconces are simple touches for this dramatic scheme. Stencils for making custom house numbers come in a variety of styles and sizes.

A jazzy color combo featuring a leaf-green door surrounded by striking lavender trim marks this door as the entry to a contemporary home. Brushed metal hardware and a one-of-a-kind mailbox are fun accents. The three-dimensional house numbers have an easy peel-and-stick application.

Rich earth tones, a wood door with a natural finish, and rustic materials such as copper and bronze lend classic character to this Craftsman-style entry door. Even the door mat—heavily textured to resemble smooth river rock—harkens to the traditional building materials of the Craftsman era.

Delightful Welcome

Here's a quick and easy flower vase to hang at your front door. There's little more to do than create a cone from wire screen material, paint it, wrap it with some copper wire, and plop in your flowers. Here's how it's done.

MATERIALS AND TOOLS:
- Pencil
- Tin snips
- Work gloves
- 2 feet of wire window screening mesh
- Marking pen
- 1/2-inch-wide fabric adhesive first-aid tape
- Wooden spoon
- Newspapers
- Spray paint in gold and cherrywood tones
- Paper clip
- Fine crafts wire
- 5 feet of 6-gauge copper wire
- Large bead
- Artificial leaves
- Hot-glue gun and glue sticks
- Needlenose pliers

1. Draw a 24-inch circle on the screen. Wearing gloves, cut out the circle. Make a cut from the outside edge to the center. Shape the screen into a cone; trim away excess. Open up the screen. Encase the cut edges of the screen with cloth tape. Rub with a spoon.

2. In a well-ventilated work area, cover your work surface with newspapers. Spray-paint both sides of the screen with cherrywood-tone paint. Let dry. With curved edge at top, roll the screen into a cone shape. Overlap the straight edges slightly, and clip the top edges together with a paper clip. Cut small lengths of crafts wire, fold in half, and insert them through the overlapped area. Twist ends together. Repeat every inch to secure the cone shape. Remove paper clip.

3. Spray the artificial leaves gold. Let dry. Glue leaves around top of cone. Wire large bead to tip. Using needlenose pliers, twist one end of the copper wire into a small loop. With your hands, twist wire into flat concentric circles around the loop. Leave the last 8 inches at the end straight. Pull the spiral up so the circles spread apart to form a cone. Insert the screen cone and adjust wire to fit. Bend 4 inches of the top out to a 45-degree angle. Use pliers to shape copper wire into a circle for a hanger. Fill cone as desired.

Trim Up That Look

MATERIALS AND TOOLS:

- Tape measure
- Hammer
- Flat pry bar
- Circular saw
- Clamps
- Utility knife
- Nail set
- Caulk gun
- Putty knife
- Sanding block
- Urethane-foam moldings to fit your doorway
- 6d and 10d casing nails
- * Adhesive recommended for your moldings
- Exterior caulk
- Exterior putty

Installing decorative trim around an entry door—whether old or newly installed—is a quick way to give your house a facelift. With the advent of urethane-foam molding, there is now a wide range of affordable molding styles to choose from.

Urethane-foam trim is light, paintable, and easy to cut and will never rot—ideal for exterior trim. The trim shown here can be purchased at a home center. For a larger selection, check online sources. You may need to measure your door and order the header— the horizontal trim piece at the top—at a certain length. The casing (the vertical trim pieces that replace the old, thinner molding) can be cut to length.

Choose a prefinished urethane-foam molding and you can clean the trim with a sponge, instead of refinishing.

1. Remove old molding. Using a flat pry bar, carefully remove old molding from around the door. Be careful not to dent the siding or the jambs; using a scrap of wood as a fulcrum helps.

2. Clear the jamb. Scrape away any accumulated paint or putty from the jamb. If the reveal line is not clearly visible along the jamb edge, scribe a reveal line. If needed, seal and insulate the gap between the jamb and the framing with nonexpanding spray foam insulation.

3. Mark header width. To establish the width of the header (the piece above the door), hold each piece of casing in place and mark along its outside edge. Measure between the marks. The header looks best if it extends beyond the casing. Add twice the thickness of the header to the overall length and mark for cutting.

Wood is beautiful, but it may be challenging to work with. Urethane-foam moldings are the ideal replacement. Light, easy to cut, and sometimes prefinished, this molding makes you look like a skilled carpenter.

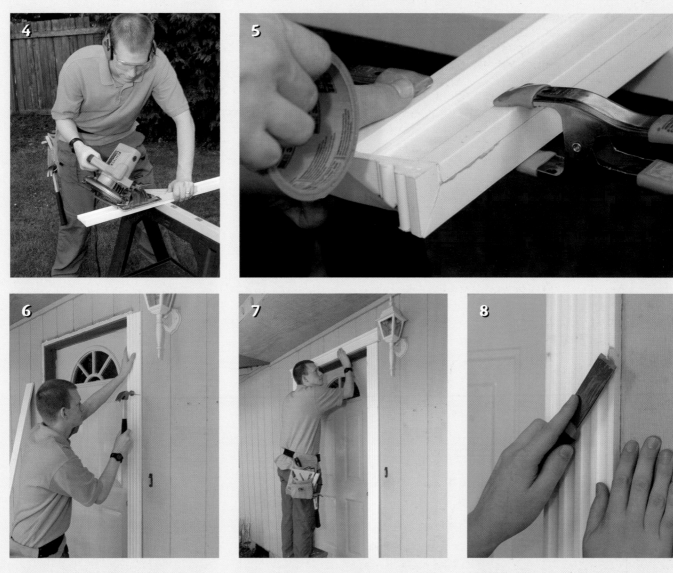

4. Miter header ends. Urethane foam cuts as easily as wood, but if the saw blade binds and overheats, a hard crust will build up. If this happens, pare off the crust with a utility knife.

5. Glue and tape parting stop. To assure that the header will stand proud of the casing, glue in place urethane parting stop along the inside of the top and bottom of the header. Cut small mitered pieces of the header to create a return. Glue and tape both pieces in place.

6. Attach the casing. Cut the casing to length. Position each piece of casing and check that it meets against the reveal line. Drill pilot holes and attach the casing with 6d casing nails driven into the jambs and 10d nails driven into the sheathing and studs.

7. Set the header in place and center it so it extends equally beyond each piece of casing. Drill pilot holes and fasten it as you did the casing.

8. Apply caulking. Set the nails and fill with exterior wood filler. Sand the filler when it is dry. Apply exterior-grade caulking all around where the molding meets the siding.

CHAPTER EIGHT

Garages & Driveways

GARAGES AND DRIVEWAYS CONNECT YOUR HOME to the street, making them entry points into your property and important elements in your home's overall curb appeal. A plain garage door and a flat strip of concrete don't necessarily detract from appearances, but adding a beautiful garage door and imaginative driveway design can have enormous positive impact on the look of your home.

The types of garage doors and driveway combinations are practically limitless. To preserve the value of your home, be sure to choose styles and designs that are well matched to the architectural style of your house. If you're considering boosting your home's curb appeal, your garage and driveway are excellent places to invest in carefully considered upgrades. Here's what to look for:

Garage style

The architectural lines of your home should guide the look of the garage. If your home is a white traditional style, the garage can be white. If you have developed a cottage look, select a design with old-world detailing that underscores the cottage theme. Whatever the style, including the garage in that look will add visual impact. Make the upgrades memorable by choosing extras such as dormers, cupolas, windows, window boxes, and attractive trim.

Garage doors

There's much more available today than plain panel doors. Take advantage of the breadth of styles and color choices, keeping in mind the sheer size of a garage door and the impact it can make on exterior design. As budget allows, purchase such garage-door options as an insulated door, windows, and automatic opening. You'll find double garage doors at prices ranging from $1,500 to $10,000.

Driveway options

Work with an architect or designer to select driveway materials that will best complement the garage style. The list of options is long, including asphalt, concrete, stamped concrete, brick, stone, or combinations of two or more materials.

The charm of a classic carriage house was the goal for this garage. It was achieved by the scale of a two-story building and by detailing such as arched doorways, overhead doors that mimic hinged doors, overhanging arbor, brick trim in the driveway, and "carriage lamp" lighting.

Gallery of Great Garages

A typical two-car garage can account for one-third of the facade that your home presents to the street. That means an attractive upgrade to the garage door probably will have a significant impact on curb appeal. As you shop for the right door package, keep these factors in mind:

- **Shop for quality.** Thicker and insulated is generally better in door materials and construction.

- **Don't always color-match your entry door.** A garage door that complements, rather than echoes, the main door is usually more appealing.

- **Add some style.** Door manufacturers offer plenty of options to improve the look of a standard panel door. Look at windows, colors, and hardware that will add the most style punch for the buck.

- **Let the pros do the installation.** Setting up the rigging, inserting the door, hooking up the electrical, and aligning everything is a major chore better left to those who know the ins and outs of door systems.

- **Add a battery backup.** You'll be able to raise the door during power outages. Add an indoor monitor to let you know if the door is open.

FAKING IT
This is an overhead door in disguise. There is only one door here, not a pair of swing-out doors as it appears. The paired handles and seams are there to fool the eye. Instead, the door raises into the garage ceiling, just like other overhead doors.

FOUR-BAR HARMONY
Vertical muntins divide a lineup of windows into a four-bar design across the top of this beaded board door. White is a good color for the garage doors when it is part of an overall trim scheme for the house. A small handle at the bottom of the door gives away the fact that this in an overhead door and not the double door those paired handles indicate.

DAPPER DOORS

Here's imposing elegance: Three smartly finished wooden garage doors that look like they would be at home in a contemporary kitchen—if they weren't so large. What's the door color? Merlot? All that's missing is a couple in evening wear.

RENEWED WITH CHARM

This garage was once beyond restoration. It was almost completely rebuilt in place. The structure was strengthened, shingle siding and brick installed. It was trimmed in new pure white lumber and a cute pair of garage doors was installed. To cap it all off, a new tile roof went on and the upper window was given some pop with shutters and a window box.

PANELS TO MATCH

Richly embossed panel doors match this brick home's accent trim. Separating doors, as was done with the brick column, is attractive and practical. The divider helps establish boundaries for two cars in a way that a single door on a two-car garage can't.

BRIGHT WELCOME

The face on each of the three custom doors on this garage is a book-matched chevron of fine wood. Though doors of such quality will require regular maintenance through the years, their stunning appearance makes the extra duty a pleasure. Dormers pop up around the roof of the garage, adding a secluded living space to the house.

ALL IN A LINE

Evenly spaced glass squares are a simple addition to a paneled garage door. Overhead, a trellis supports vines that help soften the exterior and bring attention to the door. Raised-panel garage doors in white are a good pick for a traditional-style home. The look is understated, so it complements rather than competes with the home's design.

BACK IN THE DAY

When families had carriages rather than cars, they needed room for wagons and all the gear it took to operate horse-drawn vehicles. So they built carriage houses. This brick garage mimics that style with a pair of doors fitted with metal straps. These large hinges look as though they may have been made by the town smith.

BRICK ARCHES

Here's a trick that can add architectural interest while keeping costs in check. Design door openings that are slightly arched, which will allow you to still use standard rectangular doors that come at standard prices.

Maintaining Your Garage Door

Maintaining your garage door is a simple task, but one that is easily overlooked. For years of satisfactory service, make these steps a regular part of your household maintenance routine. It's a good idea to check with the door manufacturer for specific recommendations on upkeep.

- **Keep it clean.** Wash the door exterior about four times a year using a mild detergent to remove dirt and contaminants. Don't use abrasive cleaners or harsh chemicals. If you salt your driveway in winter, try to keep the material away from the garage door because salt promotes corrosion of many metal parts. Use a rag—add a small amount of paint thinner, if needed—to clean sand and grit from tracks, hinges, and rollers.

- **Pay attention to weather-stripping.** As part of the cleaning, wipe down the weather-stripping at the bottom and sides of the door. If cracks or holes are developing, replace the strip.

- **Lubricate moving parts.** At least once a year, use a penetrating oil, such as WD-40, to lubricate movement of all rollers, hinges, springs, chains, and other parts.

- **Do a test run and inspection.** Every month or two, do a test run. Watch and listen closely while opening and closing the door. Is the door running smoothly on the tracks? Is there any binding? Are there any odd movements of the track or other parts? Are any bolts, screws, or other hardware coming loose, broken, or missing? Also, do a quick test on the safety sensors. Does the door reverse automatically if an object or person is under it? If the mechanism is not working properly, make sure that photo sensors are still hooked up and aligned properly.

Before & After Projects

Should you remain unconvinced about the style benefit of a new garage door, here's proof: four great makeovers. Originally, each of these locations was pretty vanilla, their plain-looking garage doors adding little to the design of the home. But after? The new doors have vastly improved the looks of the garages—and the houses.

New garage doors can also offer more convenience, increased security, and improved energy efficiency, particularly for homes with attached garages. A new door can pay off for your checkbook, too. A nationwide poll of real estate agents found that 71 percent believe a new garage door may add as much as 4 percent to the selling price of a home. That means new garage doors may add $10,000 to a $250,000 home.

Let the Light Shine

The undistinguished appearance of a plain, double-width garage door wasn't made any better by the blank wall on the upper level right above the garage.

Small rectangular windows along the top of the new garage door balance the three new windows on the home's upper level. The repeating pattern is simple enough to blend into the traditional home's exterior and its pillared porch.

Southern Style

A dull white garage door was a weak choice for this Southern colonial-style home. Instead of enhancing the architecture, the door softens its punch.

A line of small multipaned windows, decorative handles, and strap hinges give this garage update the 19th-century carriage-house look that the homeowners were after. The design softens some of the formality of the home's traditional style.

A Stronger Marriage

Some marriages are better than others. In this case, the garage's stark white doors don't have the visual strength needed to couple with this home's center-tower architecture.

Warm brown doors blend with the home's exterior while adding color and wood texture to the overall appearance. Vertical raised paneling plays well against the horizontals of the siding. Windows add a complementary element to the doors.

Character in the Details

There are plenty of character details in this house, including exterior trim, a tile roof, and a distinctive window style. But not much thought went into the unadorned garage doors.

Details make these new garage doors a smart design. The doors mirror the home's window style and the diagonal trim pattern above the garage. Other good ideas include strap hinges, door pulls, and outdoor lighting to assist nighttime entry.

One Day: Pick-Me-Up Projects

Think you can't make a difference in your garage's exterior appearance in just one day? Think again! Dressing up this charming detached garage took only a few supplies and a free day. Here are six small projects that will transform your garage. Hang a new sconce light. Put dentil molding on a door. Install a painted trellis. Add a basket to the door. Mount curtains inside that will be seen from outside. And plant a lush flower bed.

Gather what you need ahead of time, rather than wasting half a day on shopping. Look for supplies at your local home-improvement center and then get to work on these quick improvements. Be creative and inventive as you look for just the right pieces for your garage makeover.

Here's the garage with all six projects completed. A structure that had been a little dull is transformed into a structure that is a charming mate for a cottage-style house.

SCONCE REPLACEMENT
TASK & TIME: HANG & HARDWIRE IN 30 MINUTES
If you have an unattractive entry light on your garage, replace it with a stylish sconce. Removing the old one will reveal the existing wiring. It's a simple matter to connect these wires to the new lamp and mount it. Be sure to read the manufacturer's installation instructions and to turn off the electric circuit before you begin work. Add extra security by purchasing a motion-detector light.

DENTIL MOLDING
TASK & TIME: PAINT & INSTALL IN 60 MINUTES
Dress up a doorway by installing a piece of lightweight polyurethane dentil molding to the top of the frame. Purchase preprimed molding. Cut it to fit. Spray it with a quick-drying paint in a color that matches the frame. Once dry, apply a thin bead of adhesive to the back of the molding and set it in place. You may have to use a few finish nails to hold the molding in place while the glue dries.

PREPAINTED TRELLISES
TASK & TIME: INSTALL IN 30 MINUTES
Select trellises that fit the style you want. These could be wood, vinyl, aluminum, or another metal. Shapes vary. To keep it a low-maintenance project, do not choose a painted-wood trellis that will need regular refinishing. Because this will be mounted on the garage, the trellis can be attached to the structure.

DOOR BASKET
TASK & TIME: PLANT & HANG IN 15 MINUTES
A basket of flowers is a very quick and easy way to put some color at the door. Choose a basket or any hanging planter that has the look you want. Mount a hook at the door and put the holder in place. Fill it with artificial flowers or with soil and the real thing.

INTERIOR CURTAIN
TASK & TIME: MOUNT RODS IN 15 MINUTES
Because you want people outside to appreciate the colors and pattern, choose a curtain material that will complement the garage exterior. Select a light rod that will allow the curtain to hug the window. As shown here, you can also include shutters and a window box to put more color, texture, and detail into the setting.

LUSH FLOWER BEDS
TASK & TIME: DIG & PLANT IN 3 HOURS
Set up a flower bed wherever the opportunity presents itself around the base of the garage. Choose low-growing flowers that will give you colorful blossoms all summer long. At some point, you may want to spend a weekend putting in a brick walkway along the beds.

Dressy Driveways

Brick-Look Beauty

Even up close, it's tough to tell that this herringbone-pattern driveway is paved with asphalt, not with brick. Using 6×12-foot templates, freshly laid asphalt was stamped with a pattern. The surface was then sprayed with a colored sealer and brushed with a roller that removed excess material from grout lines and created a skid-resistant texture. Two colors were used on the driveway, including a brighter red hue for the border. Colors can be custom mixed to match most schemes.

Although a sealant helps the asphalt last longer, a new coating usually needs to be applied every five years or so. The system isn't limited to new pavement: Previously laid asphalt can be rewarmed and stamped, if it's in good condition.

Concrete-and-Stone Checkerboard

Conventional slabs of concrete serve as driveways for most of the homes in this neighborhood. But a grid of 4×6-inch New England bluestone dresses up this concrete drive so it better harmonizes with the adjacent carriage-style garage doors.

As masonry contractors poured the concrete, they left a 2-inch recess in the grid pattern where stone would fit into the slab. After mortaring the stone in place, they cleaned it with an acid wash and sealed it.

Sealing helps protect the surface. It also keeps cleanups of motor oil spills and such from leaving deep stains on the surface. Driveways should be resealed every two to five years.

Good to Know: Sealing asphalt

Although a sealant helps the asphalt last longer, a new coating usually needs to be applied every five years or so. Check annually for signs of cracks and crumbled edges that signal repairs are necessary. Catching the warning signs early helps keep damage—and repair costs—to a minimum.

3-Step Driveway Fixes

Concrete and asphalt are durable driveway materials. But cracks and potholes will always develop. Here's what to do.

Repairing Concrete

1. Widen the crack to ease filling. Use a wire brush, stone chisel, or hand grinder.

2. Remove loose material. An indoor-outdoor vacuum will do the fastest and easiest job.

3. Fill the crack with a prepackaged patching material. Wipe or squeegee off the excess. Sprinkling on a little dry concrete mix helps disguise color variations.

Patching asphalt

1. Clean out debris with a trowel, digging down to the gravel base, if possible. For small cracks that are wider than $\frac{1}{4}$ inch, use a hammer and chisel to widen the bottom of the crack so that it is wider at the base than at the top.

2. Fill with patch. For larger repairs, use a mason's trowel to draw and spread the asphalt patch from the tub. For thin cracks, apply the material directly from a caulking tube.

3. Tamp cold-mix asphalt into the patch compound, and finish by leaving the area about $\frac{1}{2}$ inch above grade. Seal the patch and the surrounding area with asphalt sealer.

Rustic Brick and Stone

This casual look is appropriate if you are developing a cottage look. Earthy bricks have a natural appeal that will make your home distinctive.

The brick must be laid on a properly developed base of landscaping cloth and sand. Be aware that some moss or weeds will likely sprout up between the bricks if you do not use a hard grout. Also, some low spots may develop, breaking the even plain you originally established. Releveling bricks is easy. With a screwdriver, pop up the offenders, relevel the sand, and reinstall the bricks.

These homeowners pointed visitors toward their entry by installing a few flat stones at the gate. Building a stone wall in the same hue as the brick was a good choice.

Brick Welcome Mat

Here's an idea that is more about design than about material choice. Homeowners here put out the welcome mat with brick. This wide brick insert in the driveway creates a spot where visitors will stop their cars, knowing they head to the front door.

At about 8 feet wide, the insert makes a strong visual statement. The tie with the house is tight, enhanced by the choice of brick in the same color as the home's weathered-shingle siding.

Bordering on Asphalt

Although asphalt is a solid choice for budgets, it does have a drawback: It's not much to look at. One way to boost the appeal is to give the dark material an attractive border, as seen here. Neatly aligned stone bricks give asphalt a tidy apron and the cut-stone walkway adds another desirable companion.

As for the budget, this approach allows the inexpensive material to carry the bulk of the load while minimizing the use of the better-looking—but higher priced—brick.

Perfectly Imperfect

Pretty as a patio, this driveway features weathered-look brick that is a charming match for the cottage it serves. To give it the casual ambience appropriate to the setting, gaps between bricks are imprecise. If a little moss grows or some soil shows in those gaps, all the better. There's a budget benefit in this approach. You can shave costs by laying the material yourself with a crew of friends. It requires some muscle, but little skill.

Catch a Wave

Energize even the flattest, plainest stretch of driveway with colored concrete put down in wavy sections. The round mosaic was fashioned from round rocks, small blue tiles, and some stone triangles. Those who park here will walk across a surfboard-shaped design as they step toward the entry. It's filled with more of the material used for the round emblem. Gridded concrete can turn any area into a geometric courtyard with the shapes and colors you want. You driveway doesn't have to look like the one next door.

A Look at Costs

A dressy driveway may not be much more expensive than one paved with conventional asphalt or concrete. As seen in previous pages, you may find that the best approach is often combining materials. Use a lot of the material that costs little and a little of that which costs a lot. The prices below are per square foot; ranges reflect cost differences based on location and/or the exact pavement style chosen.

- **Asphalt:** $1.50–$2.50.
- **Imprinted and colored asphalt** (shown in "Brick Look Beauty"): $3.50–$6.00. Source: StreetPrint, 888-581-2299.
- **Brick, installed:** $5–$7.
- **Concrete:** $3–$6.
- **Concrete with stone or paver details** (similar to example shown in "Concrete-and-Stone Checkerboard"): $5–$8.
- **Imprinted concrete** (with a paver look): $5–$8. Source: Bomanite Corp., 559-673-2411.
- **Stone, installed:** $6–$10.
- **Pea gravel:** under $.50.

CHAPTER NINE

Color & Paint

AN UPDATED COLOR SCHEME can take your house from forgettable to traffic-stopping. The average exterior paint job lasts 10 years, so selecting colors is a big decision. Most paint companies offer color cards that suggest pleasing, complementary combinations for the body of your house, trimwork, and accent pieces such as the front door. When you're ready to choose paint colors, here are the main points to consider:

- **Think about style and region.** Take into account your home's architectural style and geographic location. Give those factors weight in your color choices. For instance, earth tones enhance a desert adobe home, while Colonial blues and creams suit a seaside Cape Cod cottage.

- **Always take a long view.** The colors of certain elements of your house, such as siding and roofing, may not change for a decade or much longer. Choose accent colors that will play well against that backdrop for years to come.

- **Tricking the eye.** Remember that color can change perception of size. Dark paint can make a home look smaller and create an illusionary recession in the landscape. Light shades visually enlarge and advance a home's appearance. White will make a home look bigger and closer to the curb.

Three-tone paint always perks up an older home. Schemes like this one, with cranberry as the base and light greys for trim and shutters, are suggested on color cards from paint companies. Color experts put these historic designs together, and their advice is hard to beat.

SURPRISE AT THE DOOR

Weathered shingles bring warm browns to this cottage, but it's that entryway that grabs attention. It's not just the ocean blue door that does the trick. The stark white trim around the arched roof overhang also draws the eye.

- **Create an interesting contrast.** Two or three colors working together add life to a scene. For a serene look, go monochromatic—paint the body of your house pastel blue, the trim a medium blue, and the door navy. To boost drama, try a complementary scheme, which combines colors directly across from each other on the color wheel. Think of a white house with forest green shutters and a cranberry front door. To land somewhere in the middle, try a two-tone analogous scheme, which features colors located next to each other on the color wheel. Picture navy shutters punctuating a pale green house.

- **Give it a test run.** Narrow your color choices to two or three, then buy a quart or sample-size jar of each color you're considering for the body of your house. Brush a swatch of each on an inconspicuous spot on the back of your house. Check the painted swaths at various times of day to see how they look in sunlight and shadow.

Try these color tips:
- **If your home's exterior just looks drab** but the paint seems to be in OK condition, it may need to be powerwashed to bring back some sheen.

- **Paint the front door a bright color.** Nothing says welcome home like a cheerful entry. It's an easy, affordable way to freshen up a paint scheme without having to repaint the entire exterior.

WOODSY THEME

Since this house was built in a woodsy setting, what better color than shades of green for its front façade? A deep olive green front door was chosen to complement the pale green shingle siding. To keep the house from blending completely into its surroundings, it was trimmed in white.

BLACK-AND-WHITE FORMALITY

At first glance, you may not see much of a color story here, but look again. The dominant white makes the house seem even bigger and closer than it really is. Using black shutters helps break up all that whiteness and invests some formality into the scene. Finally, did you notice how gray was used to subdue all the shuttered windows, underscoring the brightness of the white dormers?

BOLD ENTRY
That red door became the main event here the moment it was installed. It's the first and last thing you'll notice about this modest presentation.

1232

- **Exterior trim** is extremely important to the overall look of a home. It's also the area where peeling and cracking of paint will probably show up first. So, if you see signs of deterioration in the trim, start watching conditions in other areas of the house.

- **Most houses have neutral or subdued colors** for the main body of the house. So trim is the best area to perk things up with some bolder color.

- **Paint isn't the only way to add color.** Plant a colorful flower bed or put up and fill a lively flower box. Hang flashy copper gutters. Lay a red brick walkway. Install permanently colored vinyl porch railings.

- **Natural materials also bring color to your exterior.** Short walls made of stone can put color and texture along the edge of your property or along a walkway. Wood shingles nailed up at your entry can put some faded reds, light browns, or bluish grays into the mix as the material weathers. Porch posts made from redwood can add great appeal.

ADD DEFINITION

Just because an element of design is large, that does not mean its color should be ignored. Here, vivid white trim around the window treatment makes a prominent feature even more important to the look. Imagine this same window with a light brown framing. Then the impact of the window would fade.

Good to Know: Color cues from brick

When selecting paint colors for the siding of a home that has brick or stone as a major element of the façade, take the hues of those materials into consideration as you decide on colors for trim and windows. Using the look of the brick or stone as your color inspiration will help narrow your choices for the overall paint scheme. The key is taking notice that brick and stone often have a dominant color, but there may be a muted, secondary color as well. For example, the bricks in your home may basically be red but also show some beige, gold, or gray. Use that secondary color in the material as your guide to choosing paint colors.

If bricks are red but have a beige cast, paint the trim of your home in a shade of beige. If brick or stone is used in a limited fashion, such as only at an entryway, use the material's main color for your siding and the secondary color for your trim.

The Dos & Don'ts of Painting Garage Doors

A great color scheme can make elements of a home stand out or blend in. Garage doors often look better if they blend in rather than stand out. Here's how to approach the task while avoiding missteps.

• **DO** paint garage doors in the same color as the house itself and not the trim color or white (unless white is the color of your home). Painting garage doors the same color as the body of the house will make your home appear larger.

• **DO** paint trim around garage doors either to match the door or to match the trim on the rest of the home.

• **DON'T** paint garage doors in the same accent color used on your front door or shutters. This draws too much attention to the garage and chops up the façade of the house.

• **DON'T** highlight the details of a standard garage door by painting the door in more than one color. There are historic or special doors where this may be appropriate, but for the majority of garage doors this would not be the way to go.

CALMING TREATMENT

The subdued color palette here is a good choice for the quiet architecture. Creamy yellow for the body of the house is well served by balancing it with the brown roof, green shutters, and white of the porches and trim.

QUICK APPEAL:

Here are six easy steps to getting your color treatment right:

1. Identify the looks and colors you like.

2. Scout out colors of other homes in your neighborhood.

3. Note the color of your home's fixed features.

4. Narrow down your color choices.

5. Plan the replacement colors.

6. Prep, paint, and stand back to admire your beautiful home!

Developing the Best Palette

If your house is two or three stories tall and you want more than one shade of the principal body color, it is tasteful to apply the darkest shade on the first floor, a medium shade on the second floor, and the lightest shade on the third floor. If the dark color is on top, you risk making the house appear top-heavy. Houses with shingled upper stories are the exception; these should be painted a lighter shade on the lower story.

Gutters and downspouts should be painted to make them as inconspicuous as possible. For example, on a frame house with olive trim and a light green body, the gutters would probably be olive to disappear against the olive cornice, but the downspouts would be painted light green to correspond to the adjacent siding. On masonry buildings, the downspouts are often painted bronze green to simulate weathered copper.

In climates with heavy rainfall or snow, dark-colored roofs will be more stain resistant so you'll want to choose house body and trim colors that work with gray or slate colors. Here are other paint theories about trim and windows:

• Paint all vertical and horizontal trim elements that suggest structure, such as a column, in the main trim color.

• Window and door frames usually look better painted in the home's principal body color. The same holds true for cornice brackets.

• As a general rule, it's best to make window sashes and shutters the darkest parts of the color scheme. As a result, the windows seem to recede into the façade.

• The sash color can be repeated on the front door and on the porch steps.

• Storm windows should be the same color as the sash.

• It's best if ceilings under eaves are painted in the body color, while the entire cornice—the trim facing outward—is almost always painted in the main trim color.

NEIGHBORHOOD INFLUENCE

Adding a second story to this once-nondescript house was
an opportunity to perk up the color combination. Nearby
Arts and Crafts homes inspired the exterior colors of Shaker
red, moss green, yellow, and khaki. One element was
withheld from the mix: The front door is a natural-finish
wood, boosting its presence in the façade.

Finding Colors That Last

Your color selection has a strong influence on paint performance. That's because the amount of ultraviolet (UV) light absorbed or reflected by the color affects how long a paint job will last. Dark colors absorb heat and suffer more moisture problems than do lighter shades. That's why light colors last longer and fade less than dark colors. Because dark colors fade faster, they are more difficult to touch up. When considering your color scheme, here's some tips to remember:

- Check paint-container labeling for color limitations and application requirements.

- Organic colors, such as earth tones, soft blues and greens, and light shades of tan and ochre tend to fade more quickly than inorganic colors, such as bright reds and yellows, grays, and pure white.

- Always use high-quality paints for superior color retention. Compare warranties against paint failure listed on the paint cans.

Picking the Right Exterior Paint

TYPE	CHARACTERISTICS/USE	APPLICATION
Latex	Easy cleanup, durability, and fast drying make latex the choice for amateurs; can be applied even over damp surfaces; naturally mildew-proof; may be incompatible with a previous oil-based finish.	Don't thin; apply with one stroke of the brush or roller; work it out too far and you'll get thin spots.
Acrylic	Actually a type of latex; a water-thinned paint that dries even faster than most and will cover just about any building material, including masonry and properly primed metal.	About the same as ordinary latex.
Alkyd	Solvent-thinned, synthetic-resin paint; has most of the same properties as oil-based types, but dries more rapidly; good over old oil- or alkyd-based coatings; excellent hiding power.	Thicker consistency makes alkyd more tiring to apply, but it levels better than latex.
Oil	Slow drying times (12 to 48 hours), strong odors, and messy cleanup; some professionals still swear by its durability.	Lengthy drying time makes bugs and rain real perils.
Primers	Seal new wood and metal with a recommended primer; generally, one coat of primer and one of finish is more durable than two finish coats; finish not to be used as primer or vice versa.	Priming usually is easier than finishing, but porous surfaces can soak up a lot of paint.
Stains	Solvent- or water-thinned types provide transparent, semitransparent, and solid finishes for natural wood siding and trim; some include preservatives or offer a weathered look.	Brush, roll, or spray on in almost any way you like.

Specialty Coatings

TYPE	CHARACTERISTICS/USE	APPLICATION
Porch and Deck	Choices include epoxy, alkyd, latex, polyurethane, and rubber-based paints; most work on wood or concrete floors and dry quickly; surface preparation varies; colors limited.	With most, you just pour on the floor, then work out with a long-handled roller or wax applicator.
Metal	Solvent- or water-thinned types in a wide variety of colors; include rust-resisting priming ingredients so you needn't worry about small bare spots; all-bare metal should be primed separately.	Brush, roll, or spray on for a broad range of finish effects.
Marine	Formulated for boats; provide a superdurable finish on wood and some metal trim; expensive, so not for big areas.	A gooey consistency makes them difficult to apply.
Masonry	Include latex, epoxy, Portland cement, rubber, and alkyd; some serve as own primers; seal masonry with clear silicone.	Latex is easy to apply; other types can be a lot of work.

What to Know About Paint Performance

Different types of paints offer different strengths, weaknesses, and special characteristics. One of the chief factors in the success of your project will be selecting the right paint.

Drying time and durability. Paints with oil and alkyd bases dry slowly, making them susceptible during application to insects and sudden rainstorms. Once they set up, however, they are exceptionally durable. Latex paints are easier to work with, dry quickly, and have a porous, "breathing" quality that minimizes most moisture problems. They do have a tendency to peel, however, if applied over an improperly prepared oil- or alkyd-based finish, especially if it's a "chalking-type" latex paint.

Chalking. A self-cleaning quality called chalking is formulated into many of today's exterior paints. Surfaces painted with this type of paint shed dirt by gradually eroding with each rainfall. Usually, you can see the "chalk" on foundation walls, shrubbery, and your coat sleeve, if you brush against a painted surface.

Previous coats. Once wood has been covered with a water- or solvent-thinned product, it's best not to change types when you apply subsequent coats. It can be done, of course, but you may run into problems. If you're not sure what type of paint was used before, you'll probably be safest to use an alkyd-based paint.

Luster. In addition to deciding what type of paint you want, you also must specify the luster—flat, semigloss, or gloss. (The word enamel often is used instead of semigloss or gloss.) Most people prefer a flat finish for large exterior expanses, and reserve semigloss and gloss for areas subject to hard use or for trim.

Time spent painting. If you plan to match or approximate the present color, any paint will cover in one coat. However, products sold with a one-coat guarantee are thicker, with more resins and pigments. Most guarantees specify that the paint must be applied over sound existing surfaces or primed new wood. You will pay more for a one-coat paint, but the extra money spent might pay off handsomely, especially in terms of time saved.

Exterior Paint Ideas

COST-EFFECTIVE APPEAL

Painting your home's exterior is one of the most cost-effective ways to update its look. When devising your color scheme, consider your home's architectural style—elaborate Victorian homes might be able to handle four or five colors, while Colonial and contemporary styles look best with two or three. Also consider colors that can't be changed, such as stonework on the home or in the landscape, roof color, and the palette of surrounding homes. These should help you set the tone for your own home.

COLORFUL VINYL SIDING

Vinyl siding was once offered in only a handful of neutral colors, but today's products provide nearly unlimited color choices. The rich colors available today make it easy to find siding to complement your home's exterior. Be sure to shop several manufacturers because their color shades will vary. One maker may have the darkest cranberry trim, another the widest plank, and another exactly the fish-scale shingle look you are after. Approach color choices the same way you would paint choices. Develop a balanced set of hues that will give your home the drama and style you envision.

OUTLINE YOUR SENSE OF STYLE
Cladding—an aluminum or vinyl surface for an exterior window frame—lets you have a low-maintenance covering outside while the interior frame can be a naturally beautiful wood. Manufacturers offer cladding in various colors, so you can make your windows stand out as architectural features or blend windows with existing siding, which reduces their impact on the overall visual presentation of the home. These windows are unusual because orange isn't a typical color for cladding. But by painting other window frames and some front porch columns in the same shade, the house takes on a jaunty personality.

Your front door is a great place to add bold color—and boost home value. Buyers will certainly remember it. If you are going to install a new door, look for one that comes preprimed, ready to paint. Opt for a high-quality acrylic latex paint because it's a great performer and easy to use. This water-based paint dries quickly and can be applied with a brush or roller. Paint the door with it off the hinges. Remove all hardware before starting. If you repaint an existing front door, patch cracks and holes with wood putty, if necessary, and sand thoroughly before painting. It's easiest to paint a door by setting it flat on supports at least waist-high.

A SNAPPY ROOF

At first glance, your roof may not seem to be a central player in the look of your home, but this practical element can have a big impact. For cohesiveness, choose a tone in the same color family as the paint or siding on your home—or pick out a color that repeats hues found in brick or mortar. Tile roofing comes in earthy colors, and metal roofing can add significant color appeal.

FRAME YOUR WINDOWS WITH COLOR

Whether operable or decorative, exterior window shutters add color and bring a historical touch to most homes. They are particularly appropriate for the Federal style of Colonial architecture. For easy maintenance, look for models made from fiberglass, high-density PVC, or composite wood materials; they offer the look of wood but don't crack, split, or rot. Shutters can be used as a quiet complement to the home's overall color, as they are in the image shown here. Or they can act as a stronger contrasting piece, such as black shutters against a white wall.

Good to Know: Cost of painting a house

Prices for a gallon of exterior house paint begin approximately where the cost of interior wall paint leaves off, for two main reasons. First, exterior paints contain more resin, giving them greater durability and higher moisture resistance. Second, most also have more pigment, the ingredient that gives paint its color.

If you paint new or sanded wood, apply a primer. Latex primer is $8 to $16 per gallon. Alkyd primer is in the same ballpark—$8 to $22. At $19 to $26 per gallon, oil-based primers are the most expensive. Latex paint is $11 to $36 per gallon. Alkyd is cheaper at $8 to $22. Oil paints are $19 to $32 per gallon. Expect to pay more to mix custom colors.

CHAPTER TEN

Siding & Windows

SIDING AND WINDOWS PLAY A MAJOR ROLE in creating curb appeal for your home. In the pages ahead, we'll show you how to choose replacements, add a dash of personality, and keep what you have looking great.

Once you've selected siding and windows, you've made the big decisions that will affect how your home will look and how comfortable it will be.

With siding, the choices are extensive. Siding types include wood, engineered wood, vinyl, fiber cement, metal, brick, brick and stone veneer, stucco, and synthetic stucco. Among the characteristics you will have to consider before purchase are esthetics, water resistance, ease of installation, insulation value, and maintenance.

With windows, you may choose among wood, aluminum-clad, solid vinyl, vinyl-clad wood, fiberglass, and composite. The characteristics to look for include insulation value, esthetics, durability, hardware quality, stability, and maintenance.

In both cases, it's unlikely that you will be handling installation as a do-it-yourself project. Instead, the purchase process includes research, talking to sales reps, a lot of measuring, hiring installers, and seeing the project through. Siding jobs will probably take a week or so, and window replacements are often stretched over a few weeks.

In the end, you'll probably get what you pay for. If you buy on price alone, you may not be as happy with the result as you hope to be. Instead, devote time in the beginning to deep research into what you are buying and stay with nationally respected brands that are installed by local contractors of good reputation. Read all warranties and guarantees carefully because it may take time for some flaws to reveal themselves.

Excellent choices were made for the siding and windows of this house. The multipane windows seem right for the architecture and the shingles are appealing. But the clincher is that both elements work together to create an overall impression. No matter how great a single feature is, it has to complement other materials.

ENTRYWAY OVERHAUL
A new double gable draws the eye to the mahogany front door, and natural materials—stacked Tennessee fieldstone, cedar shingles, and wood siding—complement the home's wooded surroundings. The stacked fieldstone, in particular, defines the entry, and elegant windows echo its curve.

Gallery of Siding

There are two schools of thought about exterior materials. One view focuses on the utilitarian and the other on the esthetic. The first school holds that your home is your greatest investment and maintaining its value is the only smart move. The more artful viewpoint first looks to how an exterior charms the neighbors and justifies your pride every time you come home.

Both teach the same lesson, really: Well-chosen materials are an investment that pays off. And if the choices you make balance curb appeal with energy efficiency and low maintenance, you've saved yourself time and money.

Style, cost, maintenance, and durability are some of the factors to consider when choosing siding. Fortunately, there are more options than ever.

WEATHERING TO PERFECTION
With its sloping roofline exhibiting cottagey charm, this home was an excellent choice for shingle siding. Shingles can be finished, but they are always appealing when left to weather. Over time, the appearance becomes classic. Though installation is time-consuming, there's a modern way to speed the process. Shingles can be purchased in preassembled panels so the material goes on as fast as any linear siding, such as vinyl or fiber cement boards.

TURRET PORCH

This 1910 farmhouse had a dark, enclosed, and uninviting porch. A makeover added Victorian style and more space for outdoor living and entertaining. The peaked-roof entryway and gazebo with turret roof both feature hanging baskets overflowing with shade-loving flowers.

ELEGANT UPGRADE

This house's roof was raised to add a second story with gabled dormers that extend over the porch. The front entry—previously blocked by bushes—is now a focal point. A color palette of pale yellow siding and crisp white trim, railings, and columns completes the home improvement project.

RISING TO THE TASK

The addition of an upper level transformed a standard-issue one-story ranch into a regal home. Natural-hued fiber-cement siding and white trim blend the new second story with the original bay window and entry.

ELEGANT STONE

Black granite siding sets off this home's new façade, and the peaks and valleys of the old rooftop gave way to a more contemporary shape.

Siding Types

Check materials in side-by-side comparisons using this chart. Weigh strengths against weaknesses and consider the cost as you home in on the best choice for your home.

MATERIAL TYPE	WHAT YOU NEED TO KNOW	OTHER CONSIDERATIONS	DURABILITY/ MAINTENANCE	COST
Wood	Solid wood boards are milled in several styles, sizes, grades, and finishes. Shakes and shingles are sold as pieces or attached to plywood panels to ease installation.	Offers some insulation value. Cedar and redwood species are naturally decay-resistant. Wood is flammable; look for products factory-treated with flame retardants.	Redwood and cedar last 50+ years. Leave wood to weather naturally or renew stain or paint every few years. Damaged boards are easy to repair and refinish.	Cedar boards or panels cost $1–$3 per square foot, uninstalled. Redwood costs $4–$6 per square foot, uninstalled.
Engineered Wood	Plywood or hardboard made into lap panels or 4×8-foot sheets. Sold unfinished or factory-primed. Comes in smooth or embossed textures.	Low cost. Dimensionally stable. Cuts and handles like solid-wood siding but without imperfections to work around. Cut ends are vulnerable to water damage, so need to be sealed when installed.	Warranties of 20–30 years. Will need repainting every five to 10 years, preferably with acrylic latex paint.	$1.50–$3 per square foot, uninstalled.
Vinyl	Extruded from PVC into smooth and wood-grain textures. Quality panels are at least 0.044 inch thick. Some brands' insulated-foam backing adds impact resistance.	It's inexpensive and won't rot or peel. Dark tones may fade. Not recommended for painting, so color options are limited to manufacturer's offerings.	Should last about 40 years. Maintenance generally low. Spray off annually with a garden hose. Remove mildew with household cleaner or solution of 30 percent vinegar, 70 percent water.	$1–$6 per square foot, uninstalled.
Fiber Cement	Made of Portland cement, sand, wood fiber, water, and additives. Smooth or wood textures available. Some have protective urethane coating.	Fire-resistant and termiteproof. Won't rot or crack. Resists damage from hail and debris. Holds paint longer than wood siding.	Limited, transferable warranties up to 50 years. Paint jobs should last about 15 years.	$3–$6 per square foot, uninstalled; $4–$10 per square foot with trim, uninstalled.
Metal	Aluminum or steel comes smooth and embossed with wood grain. Some codes may require electrical grounding. Steel isn't suitable near saltwater or in heavily polluted areas.	Resists fire, rot, and insects. Wide range of factory-baked enamel colors. A poor insulator. Scratches on steel siding will rust. Aluminum can dent.	Lasts about 40 years to life of building. Maintenance generally low. Check annually for scratches and dents. Needs occasional washing with a garden hose and soft-bristle brush.	$2–$5 per square foot, installed.
Brick	Classic material from fired clay. Comes in many sizes, colors, and textures. Brick needs to be supported by the foundation.	Won't rot, burn, or fade, and provides excellent sound and thermal insulation. May result in lower insurance rates. Expensive in many regions. Installation costs can be high.	Brick should last a century, with practically no maintenance in the first 25 years. Mortar joints require annual checking for cracks, which should be repaired as soon as possible.	$6–$12 per square foot, installed. Costs vary by type of brick and region.

MATERIAL TYPE	WHAT YOU NEED TO KNOW	OTHER CONSIDERATIONS	DURABILITY/ MAINTENANCE	COST
Brick and Stone Veneers	Lightweight aggregates, Portland cement, and pigments are cast to imitate brick or stone. Panels typically $1/2$–4 inches thick are usually applied to a wood-frame wall.	Wide variety of tones and styles to choose from. Fireproof; expensive. Requires professional installation. Freeze/thaw cycles and settling can weaken mortar joints.	Should last the life of the building. Virtually maintenance-free. Hose off annually.	$4.50–$6 per square foot, uninstalled.
Stucco	Traditionally, it's Portland cement, lime, building sand, and water applied in three coats over a masonry or frame substrate. Some companies offer one-coat systems.	Durable, even in harsh marine climates. Fire-resistant. Stucco on frame is susceptible to water penetration. Expensive and time-consuming to apply.	Should last the lifetime of the building. Check annually for cracks, which should be repaired.	$3–$15 per square foot, uninstalled.
Synthetic Stucco	Also called exterior insulation and finish systems (EIFS). Polymer/cement sprayed onto fiberglass mesh, foam board, or fiber cement, then topped with a textured finish.	Less expensive and less likely to crack than conventional stucco. Energy-efficient. Requires professional installation to prevent problems with interior moisture build-up.	Should last the lifetime of the building. Check annually for cracks, which should be repaired. Remove dirt with careful pressure-washing. Consider clear masonry sealer in humid areas.	$6–$14 per square foot, installed.

CLASSIC AMERICAN Architecture such as this gable-front home requires a decidedly American solution. Reddish, salvaged-look brick and cedar shingles create a charming cottage look that presents a warm welcome to visitors. Because of the design strength, this seems like a small house attached to a large one.

Adding Architectural Detail

Siding and windows play a major part in putting some polish onto this once-ordinary cookie-cutter house.

Not too long ago, there was nothing distinguished about this 20-year-old suburban ranch-style home. As you can tell from the basic shape, it was a standard-issue house presenting two gables to the world—one gable for the living room and one for the garage.

But the homeowners wanted a home with more character, so the aging cedar siding was stripped off, a slight bumpout was added to the living room gable, and shingle siding was applied. This started a transformation.

Off with the boring white trim, a dated-looking roundtop front window, and an anemically light post supporting the roof overhang near the front door. Instead, shingles and trim are the same color, which helps calm the cottage appearance. Also, the bumpout accommodates a towering bay window, and a knee-brace support post lends presence and visual strength to the entry.

The entrance was also made the star of the show with installation of a brick walkway that leads visitors from their cars right up to the door. In keeping with the charm of the home, the path meanders to give guests a moment more to take in the architecture. The finishing piece is landscaping that was carefully chosen for shape, height, and color. The redesigned home transcends its ordinary suburban roots.

MEANDERING PATH
Visitors must be struck by the simple beauty of this setting. A charming brick walkway is cushioned by a few plants and flowers, and the entry bids that all are welcome. The rich texture of the new shingle siding shows well for those who approach.

SKILLFUL WRAP
This view of the garage gable shows how the shingle-wrapped casing adds depth, dimension, and texture to what could have been an uninteresting flat expanse of siding. Note how the shingles are angled to act as a beveled window frame and how even the trim at the top and bottom of the window was given attention.

RUGGED DETAIL
The braces supporting the roof and projecting gable aren't actually carved, although that's the impression they give from a distance.

WINDOW ACCENT
The window between the porch and the garage didn't change, but adding shutters made it look wider. For another tactile element, stone veneer was added beneath the window box.

BUNGALOW GARAGE
Architectural details, such as the pergola overhang above the new garage door, brackets and braced supports, and Arts and Crafts–style lighting, soften the modern lines of the original house and imbue it with bungalow character.

Making a Statement with Windows

Windows can add a pop of amusement, button down a style, or even add a touch of romance. Oh, yes, they can fill your home with light, too.

In most cases, windows play a supporting role to the style of a home. Occasionally, however, they come to the fore and step up to center stage.

In any case, selecting the best window for an exterior design is critical to success. Of course, you want windows that add to your home's energy efficiency, are easy to maintain, and provide sunlight when closed and fresh air when open. Just keep in mind that windows should also look great just doing their job.

Here are some windows that star and some that are strong supporting actors.

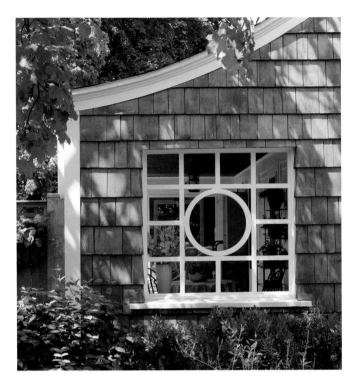

COTTAGE DESIGN
This shingled wall would have been appealing with any window. But plunk in this playful grid and the scene lifts the spirits.

EYEBROW ROOFLINE
Though almost miniature in size, window muntins in the upper level's smallest windows are a prominent feature. Simply adding a muntin at an unexpected angle draws the eye. Their companions on other windows play it straight.

COLORFUL CHARACTER
A modest story-and-a-half gets contemporary treatment and windows to match. The orange and white trim draws attention, as does the unusual treatment of the six-over-six windows on the lower level.

Window Grilles

A single-pane window starts exhibiting a specific style when thin window grilles, or muntins, are attached. Though grilles are usually less than $3/4$ inch thick, these cross members play a surprisingly big esthetic role.

In some places, they are still referred to as "glazing bars," which was their true function historically. They were developed in the 18th century as a kind of inner frame within a window sash. Muntins would hold individual panes of glass in place.

Colonial-era homes sometimes had 12-over-12 double-hung windows. In this configuration, the upper and lower sash are each made with 12 small panes of glass needing a support structure of glazing bars. There are also 9-over-9s, 6-over-6s, and other counts.

Nineteenth-century Victorian architecture brought more variety, with diamond grilles and oval windows sectioned off by muntins. Prairie School and Craftsman styles brought their own regimented patterns.

Today, new-window grilles are offered in all the existing styles and then some. You can order them in oak, pine, or vinyl. Muntins can snap on as a single piece over a large, single pane of glass—and snap out for easy cleaning. Or you can dazzle friends with true divided lights, which are built the old-fashioned way with small, individual panes held by glazing bars.

Shutter Style

If gleaming windows are like jewelry on a house, shutters function more like ties. They are an accent piece, investing a design with shape and color.

Originally intended as a device for keeping wind and storms out of a house, shutters have evolved into more of an ornamental piece. They've adapted well to their role as a support for historical architectural styles.

Paired with windows, shutters often provide a necessary splash of color or a change of texture or shape that contrasts and complements the overall look of a home.

Operable shutters are sometimes seen on homes. However, the common use of shutters now is simply for show; they are usually fixed in place.

When planning for shutters, consider size first. Determine which windows you would like with shutters, and measure those. The panels should be sized so they will cover each window. Too big or too small shutters will seem awkward. The same with shape: A square-topped shutter never looks appropriate with a curved-top window.

As for color, use shutters for contrast. They should either be the same color as the trim or some other strong element in your home's exterior. Rarely does a shutter look right if it is the same color as the dominant hue of the siding. Remember: Shutters are accents, not main players.

OLD-WORLD CHARM

With shutters open in a welcoming embrace, the dormer on this Tudor-style home certainly has no lack of character. The arched tops of these board-and-batten, solid-wood shutters fit neatly into the window's curved top.

STYLISH SHUTTER DOGS

Operable two-panel shutters bookend a window. The S-curve iron hardware holding in the bottom of each frame is a called a shutter dog. These are design pieces that appeal to many. Designs can be almost anything: playful, pretty, or formal. Some shutter dogs are fashioned as animals or stars or shells.

NATURAL BEAUTY
Modest board-and-batten shutters are companions to a window and window box. Hammered-together fir was stained and hung. Very simple.

STEP UP TO COLONIAL
Paneled and louvered shutters aren't often seen on the same house, but this Colonial Revival has them on upper and lower levels. Without the shutters, the architecture here would seem a little bald.

STORMY WEATHERED
A pair of old, imperfect louvered shutters feel right on the side of this cottage. With the shingles and lattice, the shutters have seen a few storms. But the flower box promises good days ahead.

SKY BLUE
The blue paint on these board-and-batten shutters will need to be freshened every three years or so. Good excuse to spend some time on a little outdoor project.

SETTING THE STYLE
A starchy stone residence from another era gains accessories for its windows in black shutters topped with classical molding. The structure seems formally dressed for a black-tie affair.

Choosing Shutter Material

The biggest question buyers face is choosing a material. Most shutters come in wood, wood composites, vinyl, hard plastic, and fiberglass. Here are some of the pros and cons of each material:

Wood. Remains popular because of the natural beauty and ease of making custom sizes. When well-maintained, such species as cedar and mahogany will last for many years. However, wood must be repainted or restained every few years or it will rot or deteriorate quickly. Price is moderate.

Wood composite. To get longer life from wood, manufacturers have turned to composites made with compacted wood dust treated to resist rotting. They look like and are priced about the same as solid wood, but composites generally hold a finish longer than wood.

Vinyl. With the lowest cost and a no-maintenance precolored surface, vinyl is popular. Because they are affected by heat, most vinyl shutters cannot be installed as operable. Only available in prefabricated sizes.

Hard plastic. Generally, these are made from PVC plastic. Though higher in price, this no-maintenance choice can outlast most other materials. Can be built to custom sizes, but the material is affected by heat.

Fiberglass. Durable and lightweight, this can be a good material to live with. Surfaces have a believable wood look. Material cost is somewhat high, but shutters are long-lasting.

CHOICES
There was a time not long ago when finding anything more stylish than ordinary shutters was difficult. Manufacturers offered few design choices. But in these Internet-friendly times, the range of shutter styles, colors, and hardware is truly impressive.

CHAPTER ELEVEN

Fences & Gates

A FENCE HAS MANY FUNCTIONS: keeping pets contained in your yard, defining your property line, and even adding a sense of privacy. However, a fence along the front of your property has a special role to play: it must look especially good. A front-facing fence frames your property and helps establish the architectural character of your house. A fence is a big contributor to overall curb appeal.

A front-facing fence doesn't have to be expensive to look great and be a defining characteristic of your yard. Today's modular fence designs make do-it-yourself fence construction easy and keep fence costs moderate. Home improvement centers carry many styles and types of materials, including wood, vinyl, fiberglass, and metal. Premade finials and fence pickets with imaginative shapes help give your fence distinct charm.

Like most outside features, you'll want to keep your fence clean and in good repair so it maintains its good looks. Wash your fence in the spring with soapy water, rinse with a garden hose, and paint and stain as needed. Repair or replace broken and rusted fence parts. If you have a gate, make sure hinges and hardware are in good working order with an annual inspection.

Other than great design, this fence doesn't have much to offer. After all, it's too short to keep the dog in or people out. But this house would suffer a charm deficit without the fence. Its rising and falling curves are complemented by ball-and-block post caps. Positioned for good effect, it's a character-builder.

Installing or Replacing a Fence

If you're installing a new fence or replacing an older one, be sure to keep these points in mind:

1. Do your research. Inquire with your municipal planning department and neighborhood association, if there is one, regarding regulations and covenants that dictate fencing look, height, and material. Ask about setbacks from sidewalks and property lines, and find out if your project requires a building permit.

2. Set your budget. If cost is an issue, mix different types of fences at different price points. Wood picket fencing could be placed at the front of the home, for example, connecting to chain-link fencing in the back.

3. Settle on a design. Sketch out your ideas. If you want a designer's touch, many landscapers offer planning and design assistance in addition to installation.

4. Choose materials. A white-picket fence is quintessential, but before you buy wood posts and whitewash be aware of maintenance needs. Wood may require regular refinishing and can warp and rot. Consider a low-maintenance material, such as vinyl. Other possibilities include aluminum, steel, wrought iron, and bamboo.

5. Talk to neighbors. Be open about your fencing plans, and try not to block neighbors' views. Could your new fence obstruct the view of a car backing out of the driveway next door? Take your neighbors' needs into consideration.

6. Landscape. Use trees, bushes, and flowers to mark your property boundaries and protect your home from weather and views. Remember, local building codes and neighborhood fence rules may cover such living walls.

7. Hire a pro. If fence installation isn't a job you'd like to tackle yourself, the American Fence Association makes it easy to find a local fence contractor. Visit americanfenceassociation.com. If you decide to hire a pro, ask to see examples of fences they have built.

8. Account for climate. In cold northern climates that experience frost, concrete anchors are necessary for fence posts. Posts should be secured 36 inches deep to avoid cracking in a cold snap. For warmer, damper climates, vinyl is your best material choice.

9. Provide a path. For safety and convenience, plan at least two paths into a fenced area. Ensure that one of these is large enough to accommodate bulky lawn mowers, large garbage cans, and the like. Stepping stones and pergolas can help indicate the locations of gates.

10. Add custom touches. Once your fence is in place, customize posts with decorative caps or finials. Depending on your home's style, you may want to paint the fence a contemporary color. Plant a row of flowers in front of the fence to create a welcoming façade.

PRETTY IN PICKETS
An unremarkable, small house is the last thing seen here by passersby. Instead, pedestrians and motorists will enjoy butterflies on the flower bushes along the sidewalk, admire detailing of the lattice-covered entry arbor, and be charmed by the tidy familiarity of a classic white-picket fence.

PRIDE OF PLACE

As long as there has been an America, there have been orderly yards enclosed by picket fences just like this. Building this type of fence takes more patience than skill. Since all the uprights—posts and pickets—are the same design, cutting one is the same task as cutting all. Using templates will speed the assembly-line process. To save even more time, picket fencing is available in 8-foot, prefabricated sections along with ready-made posts.

ARCH DES FLEURS

Entering from the street, visitors meander down a stone walkway bordered by bushes and proceed beneath an arching gate structure topped with vines in bloom. A similar arch and gate could be built by any moderately experienced carpenter. In just a couple of weekends, the fence could be erected and painted, making it ready to host a growing flower bush. Planted in spring with appropriate species, the arch vines could be blossoming in summer.

Good to Know: Building codes for fences

Before proceeding, check with city officials about building and zoning codes. Regulations may specify maximum fence height, distances you can build from property lines and the street, and even the materials and colors you can and can't use. Most communities offer brochures or Web sites with information about local rules. There will be special, more stringent requirements if your home is within a historic district.

A homeowner having difficulty understanding his or her obligation or seeking a construction variance may be wise to hire a design or building contractor who has experience with the local agency. Put someone on your side who's successfully navigated the bureaucratic maze.

STONE AND STRUCTURE
This type of entry gate is seen along the inland foothills of Southern California, often constructed by homeowners who gathered round stones from nearby dry river beds. Topping river rock platforms is a sturdy wooden structure with a central lamp, all in Craftsman style. The signature of this style is a love of the materials and what can be done by skilled hands.

COMPLETING THE CIRCLE
Here's a variation on the picket look: The boards are wide and the tops are cut in a sine wave pattern of rising and falling curves. The payoff is at the spot where visitors enter. Here, the tops of the double gates are cut in a smooth half-moon pattern—mirroring the rising arch to complete the circle. The skill here is in planning the cuts as much as it is in construction.

Good to Know: Picket fence calculator

When planning your materials list, try out the online picket-fence calculator at BHG.com. Plug in specifics about your fence and materials. In one click, the calculator will tell you how many pickets, rails, and posts to purchase. Go to:
bhg.com/home-improvement/remodeling/measuring-materials/picket-fencing-calculator/

How to Build a Picket Fence

You've decided on a classic picket fence and established where it will go. Begin the job by gathering tools and building materials.

For a project that will last for years, specify construction-grade heart redwood, cedar, or ground-contact, pressure-treated wood for all posts and bottom rails. These woods will resist moisture, rot, and insects.

For the upper rails and fencing, you can use less expensive grades of rot-resistant lumber. To minimize hardware rust, buy non-corrosive exterior screws or hot-dip galvanized nails.

If you want to paint or stain your fence, finish the posts, rails, and pickets before assembly. Besides saving time, you'll get better coverage.

1. Set the posts. Lay out the site to accommodate spans of 6 to 8 feet per fencing section. Dig post holes to a depth of about ⅓ the length of your 4×4 posts. Test holes to make certain they are sized correctly and located precisely by setting posts in place, starting with the end posts. Check each post for plumb by holding a level to two adjacent faces. Once leveled, attach braces to hold posts in position. Check alignment of the posts by tying a string from end post to end post, and sighting down the string. Post holes can be filled with dirt. But for sturdy, permanent installations, shovel concrete into the holes instead. Tamp the concrete to remove bubbles. After concrete dries, shape the post tops or add post caps to shed water.

2. Add rails. Attach 2×4 top and bottom rails to the posts, spanning the gap between posts. Fasten rails 6 to 9 inches down from the post tops and about 6 to 9 inches up from the ground. Nails can be used as fasteners, but noncorrosive wood screws ensure the fit will remain snug much longer. Speed installation by using galvanized rail clips, which are metal brackets designed for easily attaching planks to posts. Use a level to check for alignment.

3. Add pickets. Measure carefully and use a square to mark the location for the first ¾×6-inch-wide picket. Screw or nail pickets to rails, checking alignment with a level.

4. Shape pickets. Tie a thin rope between two posts. Use enough rope so it sags in the middle. The center point of the sagging rope should be about 3 inches down from the top of the pickets. Trace the sag line to guide your cut. Saw off the picket tops with a power jigsaw.

Making a Decorative Wreath for a Fence

A living wreath that hangs on your fence invites friends and family to admire what is really a miniature garden. Surprisingly, you can put together one of these lush decorations in about an hour.

Ricki Creamer, owner of Red Cedar Country Gardens in Stilwell, Kansas, leads wreath workshops for those eager to learn the craft. "I love these wreaths on garden gates, but they're nice anywhere," she says. "Hang them like a picture."

Each wreath begins with a 16-inch stout-wire form shaped like an angel food cake pan—a deep ring with a hole in the middle. Once lined with sheet moss, the form is filled with potting soil to hold moisture. Small plants and flowers are added, and the form is wrapped with florist's wire to hold it all together. The wire is so thin that you can't see it. Water your wreath well and hang it in a prominent place. Try a new look every year.

MATERIALS AND TOOLS:

- 16-inch wreath form
- One pound of sheet moss (available at garden shops)
- Fresh potting soil
- Two dozen small plants; try a combination of plants in 4-inch pots and even smaller plants in four-packs
- A paddle of green florist's wire (available at garden and hobby shops)

PERFECT FOR SHADE
Small shade-loving plants swirl around this pretty fence wreath. The design includes diminutive "Super Elfin" impatiens surrounded by tropical ferns of various kinds.

Soak the sheet moss well in a bucket of water and let it drain. It should be damp and pliable. Attach a short length of doubled wire to the back of the wreath form so it will be easy to hang. Place three or four such lengths evenly spaced around the back of the wreath. When the wreath is hanging, turn it

now and then to keep all the plants growing about the same length.

1. Line the form with sheet moss, the green mossy side facing out, like fitting rolled-out dough in a pie pan. Overlap pieces of moss and patch as you go. Make sure the moss overlaps both

upper edges of the form by a couple of inches.

2. Fill with potting soil. Fill the form about three-fourths full.

3. Arrange the pots on top of the soil. When you're happy with your design,

CIRCLE OF THYME

A kitchen-garden wreath planted with herbs smells as good as it looks. Delicious scents of spearmint, rosemary, and several kinds of thyme make this wreath memorable. Little violas add spots of color.

PANSIES WITH SPRING PUNCH

A pansy wreath celebrates the start of the gardening season. Bright orange and yellow pansies are the dominant plants, and they are complemented with citrus-color violas.

take the plants out of their pots one at a time and plant them.

4. Plant the sides to give the wreath a full look. Poke holes through the sheet moss in three or four places around the sides of the form, and carefully insert a plant in each hole.

5. Tuck the edges of the sheet moss back over the top, around the crowns of the plants. The moss holds the plants in place until their roots have taken grip. It also helps keep the soil from drying out.

6. Secure one end of the florist's wire to the back of the wreath form. Wrap wire around the front and back, moving in a spiral all the way around. Cut the wire and twist the end onto the form.

CHAPTER TWELVE

Lighting & Accessories

GOOD CURB APPEAL HAS VISUAL IMPACT all day long, but that doesn't mean curb appeal ends when the sun goes down. Today's delightful array of outdoor lighting fixtures includes everything from traditional sconces to easy-to-install illumination for trees and shrubbery that make your house the evening star of the neighborhood. In addition to showing off your home with nighttime lighting, you'll increase the safety and security of your property.

Although interior lighting contributes to the exterior scene, the outdoors should be considered a "room" of its own, with properly layered light. This means that there should be general ambience lighting, fixtures that put light where it will assist with such tasks as walking safely up the steps, and accent illumination that might single out an ornamental tree or other outstanding landscape feature. In addition to lighting at the entrance, it's a good idea to put fixtures at spots where people exit and enter vehicles and at steps within 20 yards of the house.

As you consider your system, don't overlook upgrading lighting controls. The newest controls enable homeowners to create a series of lighting scenes, turning preselected fixtures on and off for safety and comfort. The best part? The lights can be controlled remotely from outside or inside the house. As another option, lamps equipped with motion detectors turn on lights whenever someone approaches at night.

A compelling outdoor lighting scheme begins with a focal point. On this striking stucco home, the layout features upturned spotlights that emphasize two dramatic planter urns marking the entry of the walkway. Spots along the house walls brush the surfaces with light, calling attention to architectural details. A sprinkling of walkway lighting leads to the front door.

Five Lighting Ideas for Curb Appeal

SHIMMERING WELCOME

At first glance, a pair of large, boxy sconces seems to be doing all the work, but light from a glazed front door and nearby window adds to the ambience. For this type of arrangement, look for sconces with bulbs that work on a dimmer. You'll save energy and be able to control the glare.

SET A SCENE

A toned-down flood lamp washes a front wall to reveal the outline of the entry gable soffit. Other low spotlights give definition to more of the house and bushes. To keep the yard from fading into darkness, low-voltage rope lighting was set along the planting-bed boundary.

Good to Know: Night sky regulations

Looking up at the vast array of the heavens in the night sky was once part of daily life on clear evenings. But today, homes and other buildings are so brightly lit in cities and suburbs that the electric glow masks our view of the stars. To reverse this situation, a push for dark-sky regulations has been launched in communities across the country. Western states have been particularly active in instituting lighting rules to darken the night sky. Before planning your outdoor lighting scheme, check with your local building authority to see if there are any regulations governing outdoor lighting in your area.

BY THE NUMBERS
Make certain that your house number is well lit. Guests arriving after dark will appreciate knowing which house is yours, and emergency responders can find it faster when they can see the house number. Solar lights illuminating the number automatically light the way every night.

WAKE THE NIGHT
Switch on a new mood for your front yard by spotlighting a specimen tree or other front yard focal point. Uplighting, provided by spotlights, accentuates the texture of tree trunks and creates a pleasing glow on foliage. However, don't put too hot a spot on a tree. You just want to illuminate a few feet, not miles of night sky.

STEP-BY-STEP
Usher in safe footing on outdoor steps by installing lights in the stair risers. The soft light of these low-voltage lamps provides just enough brightness to mark each tread—and prevent glare.

Exterior Lighting Possibilities

A TWIST ON STYLE

With design flourishes that give it a horned look, this hanging fixture needs a setting with enough visual strength to handle it. Do you want a lamp to be the center of attention? If your fixture has candle-look bulbs as seen here, always find long-life replacements. Don't settle for bulbs with annoyingly short lifetimes.

LEAF MOTIF

It seems as if this lamp is held together by vines. Suspended from a short branch, the fixture has leafy fingers keeping the frosted-glass cover in place.

LIGHTHOUSE LANTERN

With its mottled glass shield wrapped with four vertical braces and banded by a single hoop of metal, this lighthouse lantern would be a suitable pick for an Arts and Crafts–style house. The fixture is a good candidate for an energy-saving compact fluorescent bulb because the opaque glass will mask the shape of the light source, even a twisty fluorescent.

COACH APPEAL

This coach-style sconce can find a happy home in a range of settings. The burnished-metal look and handsome shape are compatible with such a formal architecture as Federal and such a whimsical style as cottage.

NEW WORLD DELICACY

Visitors will admire this slender hanging lantern for the warmth of its colors and the delicacy of the fretwork. Every time it is illuminated, the glow from within will draw attention to the ornate metal casting embracing the smoky glass.

Automatic Lighting

In place of manual switches, newer technologies that turn lighting on and off automatically are making it easier than ever to light up your home and property. All are available at moderate prices.

Motion sensor. As a visitor approaches your house, the sensor detects movement and automatically switches on porch lighting. The small sensor is mounted on the fixture and can be adjusted for sensitivity to motion. For higher security, use flood lamps with a motion sensor on your garage to cover a wide area.

Optical sensor. Like the motion sensor, this sensor is also mounted on the fixture. It senses the amount of ambient light. At dusk, it will switch on lights automatically, and after dawn it will turn lights off. You never have to flip that switch.

Solar lighting. Wherever you need low, reliable light outside, a stand-alone solar light may be the best choice. You never have to run an electric line to one of these, and it will turn itself off and on with an optical sensor. Better solar lamps allow you to adjust the number of hours the light will stay lit before shutting down for the night.

Finishing Touches That Make a Difference

Adding Up Curb Appeal

House numbers are not doomed to be nondescript, utilitarian hardware that merely labels the location of your home. Give your numbers some pizzazz. Make picks that stand out from the crowd. Numbers have been designed for every type of architecture. Many more styles are available at home centers, hardware stores, architectural salvage sellers, and antiques stores. For something unique, work with a local metalworker, skille devise numbers ju

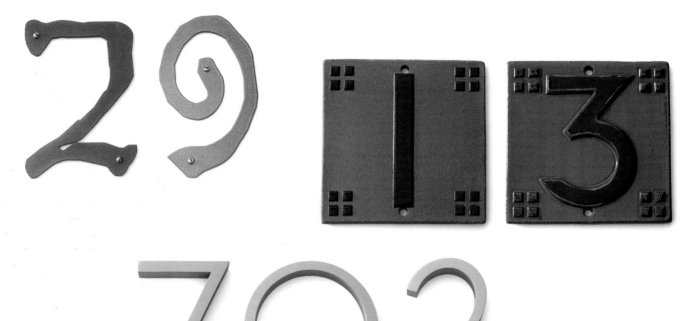

Good to Know: House numbers—how big?

Generally, numbers should be 4 to 6 inches tall for high visibility. They can be mounted on the door, near your mailbox, above your entry, or wherever you want, as long as they can be spotted easily. Avoid numerals that might rust or be difficult to clean. House numbers should be no-maintenance items.

Special Delivery

As long as it is convenient for your mail carrier, mailboxes can be attached to the wall near the door or mounted a few feet away on a short post. Regardless of where you place it, select a mailbox in a style complementary to your home. Before putting the box in, though, check with local postal authorities about any installation regulations in your community.

ALL WOUND UP

Because front water faucets may be located near entries, unsightly hoses are often one of the first things that visitors notice. Hose tenders with decorative appeal, such as the one shown above, are a good investment. A little flourish like this can turn an entry negative into a positive.

ROOFTOP ADDITIONS

A weather vane and cupola harkens to an earlier time of American residential construction, but these charming add-ons still delight. Available in a variety of sizes, cupolas and weather vanes give your roof a jaunty touch of curb appeal.

QUICK APPEAL:

Rainwater harvesting is becoming more commonplace. With drought always a possibility, wise households set up systems of gutters and large containers to capture as much storm runoff as they can from their roofs. The water can be used later for thirsty plants. A version of this basic idea includes a copper or aluminum rain chain to direct the flow of rain into barrels. Connected to gutters, chains use the natural surface tension of water to lead flows off your roof.

CHAPTER THIRTEEN

Spring Cleaning

NEVER UNDERESTIMATE THE POWER OF CLEAN. Of all the well-crafted improvements and finishing touches you might add to your home and property to make it look great, perhaps none is more impactful—and easier and inexpensive—than ensuring your house and yard are spic-and-span. An annual cleaning makes your house look great and protects the value of your property by removing from exterior surfaces any mold and mildew that may damage siding and other materials.

There are good reasons to perform this annual cleaning ritual in spring, after winter's weather has passed and a long season of exterior neglect is finally over. You'll be able to access all parts of your house and property, remove any accumulated debris, and give your house a close inspection for minor damage, such as caulk that's started to shrink or paint that may be starting to peel. Repairing those minor imperfections will save you more costly repairs later.

What needs to be done? Working from the top down, here's the typical list:
- Remove leaves, limbs, or debris if any have accumulated on the roof. While up there, inspect the condition of roofing material. If you don't need to get up on the roof, at least use binoculars to scan the condition of the material. Get repairs done, if necessary.
- Clean the gutters, check their condition, and make necessary repairs.
- Check the condition of any soffits and make repairs.
- Clean the siding and repair any damage.
- Wash any deck and railing, and refinish if necessary.
- Carefully hose off the outside housing of your air conditioner, cleaning off dirt, debris, and leaves. Make sure that the power is off when washing the unit.
- Take a rag to lighting, house numbers, mailboxes, and other accessories.
- Prune trees and bushes and clean up yard waste left over from winter.
- Wash the driveway and patch any cracks. Reposition any bricks that frost heave has moved over the winter.

A carefully tended flagstone-and-gravel walkway and nicely trimmed flower beds mark this Cape Cod–style home as an exceptionally well-cared-for residence. Note that the gleaming white trim and all the windows are spotlessly clean, giving the entire home a bright and cheerful appearance.

Cleaning Siding

After a long winter, the color of your home's siding may be muted by a layer of dirt. Give siding a good bath to refresh its appearance. Each type of siding has its own needs. Here's how:

Wood siding. Pressure washing is the usual cleaning method. If mildew is present, prepare for it prior to washing. Add about a quarter of bleach per gallon of water in a bucket, and brush affected areas with a soft-bristle, long-handled brush. When washing, you may notice that water sprayed under pressure will raise fibers from a wood surface. To minimize fibers, wash at 2,200–3,000 pounds per square inch pressure and set a heavy flow rate. Also, be careful not to raise pressure so high that it will damage the wood. For walls with horizontal siding, always clean so water will flow down the siding and not be sprayed up between slats. Water invasion behind the wood could cause rotting.

Vinyl siding. The approach is similar to wood siding: Always work from top down and do not aim water up between siding slats. First, rinse off siding using a hose with a garden nozzle set for a medium-strength stream. Then wash siding with a common dishwashing detergent diluted in water and a long-reach, soft-bristle brush. Do a large section at a time, rinsing as you go.

Aluminum siding. Clean by using about $1/3$ cup of laundry detergent to 6 gallons of water. Pressure washing is effective, but keep the pressure low so you do not dent the metal. Aluminum can also be cleaned with laundry detergent mix, applied with a long-reach, soft-bristled brush. Rinse.

Wood shingles. Cleaning solutions made for wood are best. Follow directions, which usually require brushing on solution, letting it set, then rinsing. If shingles are still dark after cleaning, test for mildew. To test, apply a solution of 1 part bleach to 3 parts water to a small area. If shingles lighten quickly, mildew is present. If there is mildew, brush on or use a paint roller to apply bleach solution to the entire area. After the solution sets for 15 minutes, scrub the area with a brush. Work the brush into the shingles' grooves. Rinse. If the shingles do not lighten after the test, tannins are causing the darkening. Purchase a wood brightener and follow the directions on the container.

Brick. Because brick is a porous material, don't saturate it with water. A light spray-off with a garden hose once a year is usually adequate. While cleaning, inspect for disintegration of brick and mortar. Repair, if necessary. If moss or algae are starting to grow, remove anything that might be blocking sunlight. This will kill the growth. If removal isn't possible, a solution of 1 cup bleach to 1 gallon water applied with a scrub brush should do the job.

Like this home, a dingy house can sparkle again after it has been given a good scrubbing with a power washer.

Stains and Other Tough Jobs

If you have steps or a porch floor at your entry, you know that surfaces get the occasional blemish. Someone spills a cup of coffee or leaf stains mar the material. Here's a handy chart with ways to remove those stains.

Removing Porch Stains

STAIN	REMEDY
Food, grease, oil, lipstick	Mix dishwashing detergent in warm water. Work the mixture into the stain with a stiff brush or broom. Don't skimp. Rinse with clean water. If this doesn't work, add ammonia to the detergent and water mixture, following the same rinsing procedures, or scrub well with mineral spirits.
Paint and candle wax	Remove all the paint or wax you can with a regular or putty knife. Scrub the area with a metal-bristle brush and cold water. If this fails, apply mineral spirits to the area. If the stain is on concrete and these treatments don't work, try aluminum oxide abrasive or an abrasive brick.
Blood, coffee, juice, feces	Use dishwashing detergent in cold water. Remove the stain as soon as possible. Work with a stiff brush or broom, and saturate the area with the detergent mixture. Rinse with clean, cold water.
Tar and heel marks	Try dishwashing detergent in warm water. If you're unsuccessful, scour the area with a stiff-bristle brush and mineral spirits. Don't use a scouring pad. If some residue remains, saturate the area with mineral spirits and blot it up with a soft absorbent cloth. This may take several applications.
Efflorescence	Rub the area with a wire brush. This should remove the white stain, which is caused by salts in the masonry mixture. If this doesn't work, many commercial stain removal mixtures are available that will remove the stain. They contain an acid, so be sure to wear gloves and safety glasses.
Dirt and grime	Hose down the surface with water and scrub it with a stiff broom. If this doesn't work, mix dishwashing detergent or trisodium phosphate with warm water and go over the area with a stiff brush or broom.
Soot	Apply detergent and water. If this doesn't work, apply a 1:1 mixture of muriatic acid and water. Be sure to wear gloves.
Mildew	Clean the surface with a commercial deck cleaner/brightener. If it is not in liquid form, mix the powder concentrate with the recommended amount of water and apply with a garden sprayer, brush, or roller. Wait several minutes, then brush briskly with a stiff brush or broom. Rinse with a garden hose. Some cleaners may contain acids or chlorine, which can harm plants; check the label.
Barbecue stains (including grease and sauce)	Scrub with a strong household detergent or water-rinsable automotive degreaser or carburetor cleaner. Rinse the area before it dries.
Tannin	Remove the black streaks of tannin-rich woods with a specially formulated tannin cleaner.
Rust	Apply a solution of water and 5 percent oxalic acid to the stain. Let it sit for several minutes, then rinse.
Leaf stains	Spot-scrub the area with a 1:1 solution of household bleach and water.
Green algae or moss	These stains are difficult to remove and usually reappear once the roots are formed in the wood, but you can temporarily eliminate them by scrubbing with a solution of 4 parts bleach to 1 part water.
Sap	Scrape excess material with a putty knife or steel wool. Wipe with turpentine.

Cleaning Specific Concrete Stains

Many everyday stains have everyday solutions. There are even plans to follow when stains are as tough as oil on concrete. Try these recipes for a cleaner household.

Accumulated grime. When you move a flowerpot that has been on a concrete surface for a long time, you will likely see a colored circle where it sat. Concrete also often turns dark from airborne grime that builds up as it settles. A portable, high-pressure water sprayer is an excellent tool for cleaning these types of problems from driveways, walkways, and patios. A stiff brush, soap, water, and elbow grease also work.

Embedded stains and rust. Various heavy-duty, acidic cleaners are available that will remove the toughest stains from concrete. Be aware that many cleaners—if the cleaner is not diluted or otherwise used improperly—can damage concrete as well as clean it, particularly smooth-finish concrete. Test the cleaner in an out-of-the-way area first. Follow directions carefully.

Oil and grease. Commercial stain removers, available at hardware or automotive supply stores, effectively clean oil and grease stains on concrete. Typically, the powdered, liquid, or spray-on chemical is spread over the stain, allowed to penetrate for a few hours, and hosed off. Using a high-pressure hose nozzle speeds the removal.

Moss. Moss will grow on any outdoor concrete surface that is moist and shaded. Pouring boiling water over the moss usually kills it, though this may not be practical for a large area. Full-strength laundry bleach is also effective. Swab it over the area with a mop, but be sure to wear rubber boots and old clothes. Rinse thoroughly afterward, and wash off any plants that may have been splattered.

Moss-killing products containing iron, zinc, or fatty acids of potassium salts are also available. Look for products labeled for most control on concrete. Follow all product directions.

For best results, seal the concrete after treating it. Moss will grow back but will be easier to remove.

You don't need a delicate touch when power-washing concrete. Use a 3,000 pound-per-square-inch unit with a rotary nozzle and a flow rate of at least 4 gallons per minute. Chemical-cleaning additives help, but check water run-off restrictions in your community first.

Cleaning Gutters and More

When you consider that your roof's drainage system may annually divert thousands of gallons of water away from your house, you can see why it merits a semiannual inspection.

Check gutters and downspouts every spring before heavy rains begin and late in fall after leaves have fallen. Remove all debris that is clogging the system, look for rust or corrosion, and be vigilant for low spots where water may be standing. Because standing water causes most gutter problems, make sure the gutters slope toward their outlets. To check this, pour some water into the gutter and watch what happens.

Eliminate sags by lifting the gutter section slightly. Look for and repair loose hangers, or bend up hangers with a pair of pliers. If this doesn't do the trick, install additional hangers.

Here are steps for your annual gutter work:

Remove debris. Debris clogs up gutters and downspouts, and holds moisture that causes rust, rot, and corrosion. Fasten a metal angle to the end of a long pole or board, then use it to rake debris toward you. Other methods for removing debris include purchasing a gutter-cleaner wand that attaches to a garden hose or trying out a motorized gutter cleaner.

Wash out with a hose. Hose your gutters clean, beginning at the high end of each run. If the run has downspouts at both ends, start in the middle.

Blast out blockage. Water pressure or a plumber's snake can push out a blockage. If not, you may need to dismantle the downspouts.

Scrape gutter clean. If the inside of a gutter is rusting, clean it with a scraper or wire brush, then apply a thin coat of roofing cement.

With spring, out comes the ladder. There's no better way of getting gutters in order than a close inspection so you can remove every bit of debris. While you're up there, check for any gutter problems and make necessary repairs.

Good to Know: Removing paint from brick

Brick is porous, making paint removal difficult. When paint residue is a problem, first scrape away as much as possible while doing minimum damage to the brick. Go easy because brick is actually a fairly soft material.

Once you have the easy paint removed, test a paint stripper on a small, unobtrusive part of the brick to make sure it will not stain the brick. If the chemical works, apply stripper to the remainder of the affected brick.

Top 10 Yard Clean-Up To-Dos

With longer, warmer days lifting your spirits, it's time to get outside and get the yard ready for viewing. Here are 10 items to put at the top of your list.

1. Debris. Walk around the house picking up the papers, cans, old toys, and any other trash. As you circle the house, watch for cracked glass on basement windows, gutter problems, signs of frost heave, and other items that you'll need to correct.

2. Dead plants. Remove and plan replacement for any plants that died over the winter.

3. Crab grass and weeds. Spring ground is soft for digging, so this is a good time to tackle areas that are overrun by weeds. After cleaning out, line the area with plastic liners and wood chips or take other steps to upgrade the area.

4. Overgrown limbs. Bring out the pruning tools to get rid of unsightly branches.

5. Edgings. Closely inspect the borders between various areas of your yard. Over winter, edgings may have lost definition as ground covers start to overgrow and pebbles along a driveway start to cross boundaries. Reestablish order.

6. Bricks and stones. Frost heave is a problem in many geographic areas. If any brick or stonework placed in the ground shows signs of movement over the winter, dig up the affected material, level the foundation, and reset.

7. Grass. Feed and, if necessary, reseed the lawn to green it up. This may not be cleanup, but it is a necessary spruce-up to maintain an appealing yard.

8. Sidewalks and walking paths. Sweep and wash sidewalks and walkways.

9. Fencing and wood structures. Use a hose sprayer to clean fencing, arbors, and other yard structures. Repair any damage to pickets, lattice, and such. If necessary, put painting on your weekend projects list.

10. Yard lighting. Check yard lighting for damage and replace any bulbs or fixtures if needed.

Index